Home

Poetry

USA Today
Bestselling Author

UVI POZNANSKY

And Poet

ZEEV KACHEL

Published by Uviart
P.O. Box 3233 Santa Monica CA 90408
Blog: uviart.blogspot.com
Email: uvi.author@gmail.com

First Edition 2013
Printed in the United States of America
Book design, cover design, and cover image by
Uvi Poznansky

Contents

Uvi Poznansky

Poems and Prose

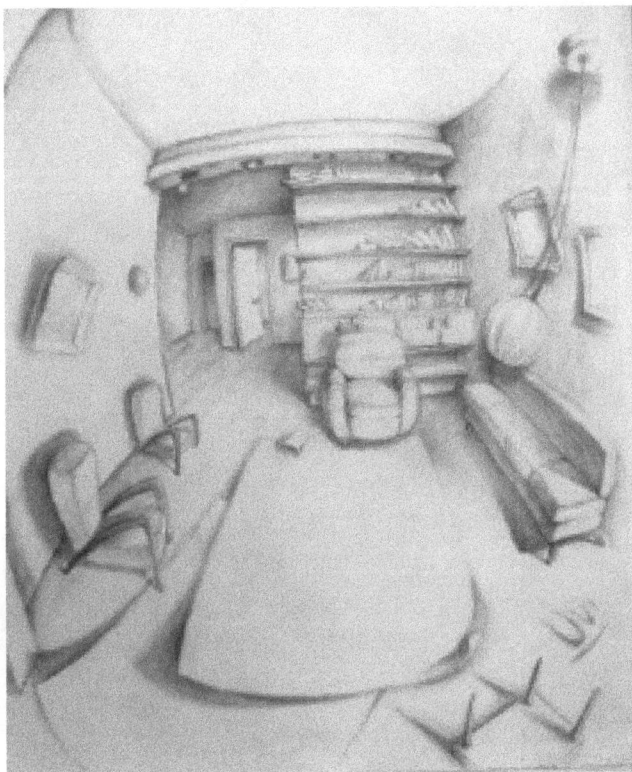

Home

Uvi Poznansky, 2012[1]

S ucked in by a force, I'm flying through a tunnel

The tunnel of memory that leads me back home

The past blurs my present, so my vision is double

The walls and the ceiling curve into a dome

From here I can see my home, tilting

And falling from place, all the lamps are aflame

My father's empty chair is slowly ascending

Tipped by the light, outlining its frame

---

[1] This poem, and the two poems immediately following it, were inspired by Uvi Poznansky's oil painting *My Father's Armchair*, displayed on the front cover.

This is the Place

Uvi Poznansky, 2012

T his is the place where he put pen to paper...
   But clung to the wall, the shelves are now bare

All that remains of his words is but vapor

All you can spot is but a dent in his chair

He used to sit here, here he would stare

Years come, years go, an old clock keeping score,

He would scribble his notes, crumple them in despair

Waiting for his savior—but locking that door

That door sealed him off, away from all danger

Except from the depth of the danger within

No one could intrude here, except for the stranger

Who would carry him off to where his end would begin—

The poet, who'd mourned the loss of his mother

Would then, somehow, be reduced to a child

He would crouch at the threshold, and call, call, call, call her

Knock, knock, knock at the door; no more held back, but wild

Home

This is the place where he put pen to paper

Till the door opened, creaking on a hinge...

Locked in embrace, perhaps at last he can feel her

No need to cry now, can't feel that twinge

Muse

Uvi Poznansky, 2012

T he lamp swings like a pendulum

                    Pictures sway on their nails

Then slip down the walls, leaving scratched trails

Amidst the quake, the grief, the confusion and scare

Slowly ascending is my father's armchair

And beyond all these outlines of what I see there

Beyond the sofa, the knickknacks, the old furniture

Light pours in, and it paints something new

It reveals, it unveils at this moment a clue

The clue to a presence only he could once see

A presence he longed for, because only she

Could call him back home, and envelop him so

Touching-not-touching, her hands all aglow

These pages, upon which he'll never scribble a line

Are floating out of shadows, into the shine

Only she can now read the blanks, she and no other

He's ascending into the arms of his muse, his mother.

A Sentence, Unfinished

Uvi Poznansky, 2004

At this moment, a man is lying in his armchair, propped up on a large pillow. He has lived, or rather, has confined himself within these walls for decades, for a reason unknown. In this stagnant place all sounds are muffled, all images erased—but for one thing: his youth. There is a vibrant longing in him for the adventures of his early days.

Was it not just yesterday when he left his home in Poland, never to see his parents again? Has he not escaped from the Nazi death camp in France, climbed across the Pyrenean Mountains, and found his way to Spain? He can still spot the snow-covered trail winding down, shining in the mist. It is fading out now, vanishing into a cloud, into fog.

No, it is not fog anymore but a storm, a raging storm at sea. There he stands, aboard the deck of a small ship, straining to see the dreamy outline of a new shore: Israel. There is a certain glint, the vivid, restless glint of the wanderer, playing in his eyes.

It is high noon, but the room is dark. The blinds are drawn. Only a thin plume of daylight reaches in somehow, and writes a bright dot against the shadows. If—like him—you waited long enough, you could actually see the dot bleeding slowly, steadily across the bare floor, rising up over the wall, becoming longer and longer still, until at long last it would fade out, like a sentence unfinished.

Dark circles can be noticed around his eyes; which suddenly brings to mind a tired animal, one that has not felt sunshine for a long time. The eyelids fall shut and at once, the glint is gone. An invisible hand is writing on the wall. He knows it in his heart. He bears it in fear and silence.

And then, trying to ignore the ticking, the loud, insistent ticking of the clock from the adjacent kitchen, you too would, perhaps, start sensing a presence. Voices would be coming from a different place, a place within. A faint footfall... A soft laughter... Who is there? He glances nervously at the entrance door. Is it locked? Can a stranger get in? Then—quite unexpectedly—the fear subsides and for the first time, gives way to something else. Something wells up in his throat. Why, why is the door locked?

He feels a sudden urge to crawl down, get to that threshold, and cry. Mommy! Open the door! Let me in, mommy! Let me come home! But for now, he can still hold it in. He forces himself to turn away from that door. Somehow it feels lighter in the dark. The bareness of this space, which was once adorned with rich Persian rugs, colorful oil paintings and fine furnishings, is more bearable this way. So is the weight of loneliness.

Opposite from him, playing out endlessly, unintelligibly and in quick succession on the TV screen, are strange images from unfamiliar places. Noise. He lets the images come. He lets them go. He has no will. He has no curiosity. But from time to time he stirs, despite the sharp, sudden pain in his wrist. He fumbles at the remote control, wondering why the sound is so distant, so mute. And yet—no matter how much he tries—he finds it impossible to fix that which is broken. The shelves behind him are laden with books, three of which he has written himself in years past. Signed: Blue Wolf.

Here is the poet, a man notorious for his contradictions, a man of a great passion and an equally great skill to capture it, to put it in beautiful, eloquent words in any one of ten languages. Here is the storyteller whose listeners have left him. Locked in a world of no sound, in a world of no expression, here he is: a cage within cage. This is the place where even the wolf surrenders. The fight is over. No more howling.

Here, at last, is my father.

His First Home

Uvi Poznansky, 2004

ere is the place—he can bring it back—his first home. Straight ahead is the door with a big handle high above. He can easily reach it, standing on the tips of his toes and pushing, pushing forward. It opens! Here is the room, which he shares with his sister, Batia. He is three yours old; she is five. And somehow he knows: she will come in later, much later. He can climb into bed now. Sleep is coming; he can feel it. Sleep is almost here.

It weighs heavily on his lids, but—for just a second—he can lift his dreamy gaze and look up at the painted ceiling. Half of it is *night*, with a large crescent moon surrounded by a swirl of stars, the other half— *day*, with a bright, yellow sun. He rubs his eyes, astonished. Nothing like this has ever happened before: They stir! The sun, the moon and the glowing stars—they all seem to move, seem to turn overhead...

Then, all of the sudden, amidst the glow, he finds himself standing at the banks of a lake with his daddy. He lets go of his daddy's hand, flings a stone and at once he can spot—right there, in the middle of the lake—a ripple taking shape. One circle rises magically inside another, widening, riding out farther and farther until at long last it fades out. White lilies can be seen floating all around. One of them is right here, at arms reach. Only a thin line, the line of illusion, separates the petal from its white reflection. And underneath it, schools of golden fish scurry in one direction, then take a sharp turn and flow elsewhere.

And from somewhere in the distance he can hear a shrill sound: the whistle of a train. Soon, Zeev knows, it will go out of earshot again, as the train travels past the hills, going away on its mysterious journey, calling him to come, calling him to follow.

A Child on a Wagon

Uvi Poznansky, 2004

There he sits, pressed in between bundles and things that keep rattling around him, on top of a horse-driven wagon. Looking up at his parents he can sense something big, something fearful and unspoken casting a shadow over them; and they bend their heads together over him and his sister. He can see an endless line in front, an endless line in back—horses and wagons, wagons and horses as far as the eye can see—all advancing towards the same gray, unclear horizon, all escaping towards the same destination: Unknown.

The sun rises in front of the wagons, and sets behind them. Towns appear and disappear. Rivers pass by, then forests, brick houses, motels. In Minsk they stop. He finds the three-story hotel quite fascinating at first, especially the curved rail of the staircase, which is meant, no doubt, for sliding down and yelling at the top of your voice. Of course, landing down on your butt, he finds out, is an entirely different matter—and so is the harsh, unforgiving look cast down at him by the hotelkeeper.

They settle down for the night. In the rented room, his mommy blesses the Sabbath candles. Her hands are tightly clasped, her eyes closed. And early the next morning they mount the wagon again, and the journey goes on in the dim light, guided by nothing but an instinct to survive, farther and farther away from home. Squinting at the rising sun, Zeev finds it more and more difficult to keep his eyes open. His mind is going numb listening to the wheels as they spin and turn, spin and turn, beating incessantly against the mud.

Cold rain starts coming down at him, sheet after sheet, and streaming in the same direction is the wet mane of the horse. Its head keeps bobbing up and down, up and down in front. When will it end? Where can they go?

Many days pass by—he cannot count them any more—until, one evening, as they travel along the river, a big town comes into view, closer and closer against the smoky blue backdrop of the Ural Mountains.

This, his daddy tells him, is Saratov.

*

My father was born 1912, and the story above is how I imagine the story of the family, escaping their home on the eve of World War I, which started on August 1, 1914 with the German declaration of war on Russia. Always an army town, the fortress of Brisk was now flooded with Russian military personnel, and many private houses were requisitioned to accommodate them. Late in July 1915, with the installation of new hospitals in town, it became clear that the front was fast approaching Brisk De-Lita.

Rumors of evacuation were heard and the Russian army was to fortify the east bank of the Bug River; but when the German army captured Warsaw on August 4, the Fort Commandant gave the civilian population in Brisk three days to evacuate. Imagine the panic amongst the Jews, who owned most of the businesses, when they had to abandon their belongings and flee for their lives.

When the German army marched into Brisk on August 25, it was a town without people, but with a great abundance of merchandise in the stores. And on the eve of Yom Kippur, the 18th of September, they entered Slonim, a neighboring city, and pressed on into Russia. By that time, the family was already far away from the frontline.

A long, dragged out journey had begun.

A Heartbeat, Reversed

Uvi Poznansky, 2010

It was a childless marriage, childless by choice; his choice. A choice about which she had no misgivings, usually; or, if she had any, Edna would soon forget them in his arms.

Leaning her head against his broad shoulders, she would take in his smell, a mixture of shaving lotion and a trace of sweat, and think herself happy.

But tonight she was lonely. Ethan was not there. Edna tried to imagine him coming close, even whispering some sweet nothings in her ear. She waited for the whisper to dissolve, then tried to force another one—but again, the voice was vacant. She rose to the tips of her toes, as if longing for a kiss. She could almost feel him. His embrace was tight, she nearly fainted—but there was no breath, no warmth in his lips. It was, to her, like a kiss through a handkerchief.

Is it too much to ask, to be protected by a strong man, to be desired? To be adored, even pampered? Edna held her breath, thinking she heard someone at the front door. She ran excitedly through the corridor to meet him; but no, there was no one there. On the way back she caught sight of her reflection, hanging there in the mirror.

For a second, it looked like her older sister. Edna stuck her tongue out at her, thinking, oh well, those wrinkles are just a play of shadows, just shadows in the murky glass. She could make them disappear, simply by tipping her head backwards. She leaned over the cabinet for a closer look. The eyes looked somewhat blurry; so did her mouth. It seemed like a smudge, perhaps because the lipstick had been wiped, or else because she was too close.

In her youth, she was so weak that she could easily fall for something, easily laugh for anything. But that other woman, on the other side, seemed as if she could easily cry for nothing.

There, see? She rubbed the corner of her eye. So did Edna, thinking it was hard to know, anyway, if someone was crying or laughing. The features of the face contorted in much the same way.

There were walls around her, on both sides of the mirror; walls waiting for something to happen, for anything really; waiting there with great patience—with stability—as if they were home. Edna looked away, unable to escape that feeling, the feeling that there was no motion, it was all an illusion; and that in reality, both she and her reflection were absent. She was lost and could not be found.

She counted the beat of her heart, counted it aloud as if she were a child, a small child playing hide and seek. Nineteen... Eighteen... Seventeen...

When, she asked herself, will he come? Will he ever come? Will he be looking for me? I am not here. I am not there. Not anywhere. I cannot be found.

It would be impossible to sleep tonight. She thought about the frequency of his business trips, which for some reason had increased lately, and decided that if he came in just this minute, if he called her name, she would stick her fingers in her ears, pretending she could not hear him.

I cannot hear you! I cannot hear you...

She became increasingly more anxious, opened and closed several drawers, shuffled some supplement packs, some medicine bottles from here to there. These wrinkles are no shadows, Edna said to no one in particular. Given time, they will deepen, spread, gain more hold, more definition. Time must be stopped. I cannot grow old, cannot waste away.

It is too frightening, really. I must stop wasting my time. Stop wasting it using cheap, old remedies.

Tomorrow, she decided, she would allow herself to splurge: Yes, she would buy that expensive, celebrity endorsed anti-aging miracle cream, which contained powerful moisturizing agents; these had sensational skin firming effects. The thought of it made her cheerful. She could be young again, tomorrow.

She pushed hard against the drawers, even though they gave some resistance, and the second she shut the last one, something creaked and the cabinet doors flew open. She peered inside and could see, deep down on the bottom shelf, a box. It smelled of dust, of forgotten things. What she was about to discover would move her life in an entirely new, unexpected direction.

She pulled the box out and lifted the flap, under which was a thing, a hard thing covered with an obscure plastic wrap, through which she could already recognize what it was: The silent movie projector, which she had used frequently until moving to this place, nearly thirty years ago.

Now Edna recalled how the very act of projecting had been a special ritual, a special game for her: Watching the reels turn, listening to the sound they produced, gauging the contrast between the blackest black, the whitest white—and above all, playing with different speeds, both forwards and back. It made her marvel at how the brain would merge separate images, to create the illusion of motion.

Giddy with excitement, Edna carried the box to the living room. She used her elbow to clear the coffee table and then, very carefully, set it down. Inside, tucked under the machine, she found two reels: One empty, the other heavy with celluloid. The filmstrip rolled down her fingers. Thrilled at the familiar touch, the touch of perforations, she threaded it as best she could, up and down through several guides, until it locked into place. Then, aiming the projector at the wall, she fired it up.

At first, it stirred into motion, casting a glowing, larger-than-life face into the darkness. The eyes sparkled, and from the lips came a laughter. It was giggly, yet utterly silent. Edna smiled back at this girl, the spirit of her youth. The eyelashes fluttered and then—with a sudden stutter—something took over the machine; for stuck on that single frame, it started rattling uncontrollably.

Even worse, Edna noted something strange about the image. It was disrupted in places by some small, underlying things, some pictures which—in her haste—she had neglected to remove from the wall. Right there between those eyes, which were as big as lampshades, hung an old picture of her, locked in arms with her pregnant sister; and under that forehead, which was as wide as the entire room, hung another picture, showing three of her sister's grandchildren. Looking at them, Edna felt empty. Empty and barren.

She rose to her feet, took the pictures off the wall and stared blankly, for a moment, at the nails. Standing there with her back to the light, her shadow sharpened, cutting into the image. There was no motion. Stop. She turned off the machine. Something was wrong. There must have been some mistake in the way she had set things up.

Edna studied the two reels: One empty, the other heavy with celluloid. It occurred to her that they were suspended like scales between joys and sorrows. Like herself and her sister, they could achieve balance—but only when they were both empty.

She should start by rewinding. This way time would start ticking, ticking in reverse: As if she were running back the clock, regaining her youth, her lost opportunities.

Edna looped the filmstrip again, properly this time. A number appeared in the darkness, vibrating on the wall, right in front of her: Ten... Nine... Eight...

In a flash, up there between those two nails, there she was: A fragile doll, dressed in a flowing wedding gown trimmed with pearly white lace. Suddenly, rising behind her was a large, tilted shadow.

It was him; every motion—reversed. Ethan gathered her to his chest, his face dark with effort, his brow dripping with sweat. He swept the bride off her feet, and carried her in his arms, walking backwards. He backed away from the living room, out through the corridor. Edna shouted, Look out! She sucked in her breath; somehow she was quite sure that in a snap, the veil would ensnare him.

And indeed, it did. Ethan nearly stumbled—but then made it, somehow, across the threshold. You could see him framed by the door, his outline dark against the streetlights out there. He balanced his burden, and climbed down a flight of stairs without a snag, and without toppling over. He managed to hold the bride steady—more or less—and must have felt lucky, for he did not even bother looking down at the next stair behind him.

By the time he had reached the landing he was no longer perspiring; neither was he breathing heavily. Like an army in retreat, he became lighter on his feet. All the while, clinging to him for dear life, the bride kept smiling pretty, as if oblivious to perils of moving in reverse.

She surrendered nothing, not a hint of distress—but looking at herself, Edna wanted to cry, Stop! Let me down! At which point the clip came to an abrupt end. Without missing a beat, a new one began.

In this scene, the bride was facing a group of her girlfriends. She opened her arms to them; but the girls stayed shoulder to shoulder, frozen and remote. From afar, they seemed to be giggling at her. Then —without warning—one of them raised her hand, took aim and thrust something directly at her.

Into her arms it flew: A huge bouquet of roses. Before Edna could move, before she could say, "No, don't," the bride clutched it. She pressed it to her breast and—with tears in her eyes—kept smiling pretty. She took a little step back, a little stumble, which suddenly blew ripples in her wedding gown. A drop of blood lifted from the lace. It squirted up as high as those fingers, where it glistened for an instant; and then, evaporated into thin air.

The bride took a deep, sensuous breath, smelling the sweet fragrance as if she had already forgotten the pain, forgotten the thorn lurking there, underneath the rosebuds; at which point—like a memory—the scene gradually faded.

The next scene opened with black leaves floating across the surface. No, not leaves but rose petals, some of which had already started to wither. They were swaying, scattering all over, all around her feet, making her feel unstable. Edna whispered, let it pass. Let it be over, soon. The moment was ripe with tension:

Ethan and the bride had just separated out from a kiss and stood still, facing each other. The silvery light could barely filter through the wedding canopy. Gathered around them were members of both families. They bore witness, in a serious and ceremonious manner, to the unravelling of this union.

Edna could see clearly how he kept tugging at that ring on his finger, as if it did not fit, no, it did not feel quite right, now did it. She caught herself hesitating, wavering there under the gray shade, between one nail and another. Finally the bride took back her vows and set him free. With great gentleness, she recovered his ring. Ethan, in turn, recovered hers.

The scene started fading, as if white veils were falling, one layer over another, over her. She held on to her sister, and started circling around him. Seven times she circled, as if rewinding a filmstrip.

Seven... Six... Five...

In a daze she backed away from him, tracing her steps back into her own footprints, erasing them; erasing herself. Glistening in the fog, rose petals drifted across the path. One by one, they were plucked from the air, from the ground, from soles of shoes and hems of dresses, and heaped into a basket. Keeping in step behind her sister, the bride withdrew even farther.

The wedding canopy shrank away and after a while, vanished into white mist. So did he, he whose name she forgot.

Her eyes fell shut—but only for a moment. She opened them and was surprised to see, somewhat out-of-focus, her sister looking at her, lips moving. There was no sound; but even if there were, Edna knew the words would come out garbled, as the syllables would surely clash, if uttered in reverse. Yet by the sight of it, she could suddenly recall that conversation, which had taken many years to forget.

Her sister gazed at her with moist eyes, saying, "Look at you! How radiant you look today!"

To which the bride begged, "Say you don't hate me?"

"Why should I hate you? It's over now. He is yours. He is no longer mine."

"But I love you. Really, I need you—"

"You need me for one reason, and one reason only: To baby you."

"Oh stop! That's a lie!"

"From now on, it's his turn. I do wish him luck."

"And me, what about me? Wish me luck, too!"

"What a pity," said her sister, in a rare moment of cruelty. "You do not have what it takes to become a real woman."

Edna grew sleepy. The scene went blank before her eyes. She could hear, faintly at first, the mechanical hum of the projector. It went on faster and faster, spinning its reels—but at this point she could not make up her mind whether she was dreaming or not. There she was, lost in the middle of a strange story; her life, rewinded.

It felt like evening, noon, morning, and suddenly night again; winter, fall, summer, and suddenly spring again. Edna touched her body. It seemed more agile, more slender. A change was upon her; she could sense it despite her drowsiness. She turned over. By some strange twist, she fancied that she was suddenly flat chested.

Curiously, the sleepier she became—the more her body awakened. It ached with desire. She must have boxed up this feeling and now, it could no longer be denied. To her surprise, there was a certain tenderness in her nipples, such as she had not felt in a very long time —ever since her early teenage years, come to think of it.

Edna could hear the sound, the maddening sound of celluloid sliding across and over itself; like air sucked in, whistling between the teeth. It made her head reel. Scenes raced through her mind in quick succession. This was no longer a game: She was helpless to stop this mad rush, a rush towards something unknown, towards the beginning.

People came in and out of her life: Men, women, children, all of whom she had long forgotten. They were not the least bit embarrassed about walking in reverse, like circus acrobats on a tightrope. For the most part they managed to do it without bumping against each other or taking a fall.

Like prunes in water, old men lost their wrinkles and gained back their plump skin. They spat out their medicines, and were instantly healed. They promised her love—love for eternity—but soon after, started to backpedal. Middle-aged women became young again, detaching themselves, in the process, from one boyfriend after another until even the first one backed away. Then they found themselves turning into wide-eyed virgins.

Children became smaller. They forgot all their words, cried longer, the pitch of their voice rose higher and higher until finally slapped by a nurse; at which time—guided by an umbilical cord—they disappeared into a void, into their mother's womb.

The prospect of finding the end of life at the beginning seemed contradictory at first; but then, she figured, it was so much better than finding it at the proper end. It would be scary, either way—but when time draws near, you need all the help you can get. At least, as a baby you are cute, irresistibly so; which makes people want to take care of you. Not so when you are old.

Edna slipped to the floor and cuddled herself. The machine kept on humming above her—but at this point she had no idea how to stop the thing. She turned her attention to that other sound, which echoed around the room: The beat, the wild beat of her heart. A heartbeat, reversed.

Then, in the distance, a scrape could be heard, like that of a key, yes, a key turning in its lock.

The front door opened. A sudden gust of air blew in, carrying an unfamiliar smell, a mixture of shaving lotion and a trace of sweat. Someone stepped over the threshold. He walked forward, which by now she found rather unusual, maybe even disturbing. Why won't he stop? Why won't he reverse his course?

When will he go? Will he ever go?

The thud of his footsteps came to her, closer and closer, louder and louder through the floor boards. It startled her, but she had no wish to open her eyes. Edna curled over her knees, and listened. Her heart was pounding so hard, so fast! Could he hear it? How could he not?

Willing her heart to slow down, she tried to relax, tried counting it down. Before she knew it, she found herself so close—so terribly close—almost there, at the beginning. Three... Two... One...

"Where are you," he cried out playfully. "Come out, come out, wherever you are!"

I am not here, she said to herself. Not there. Not anywhere.

He passed through the corridor, calling, "Where are you? I cannot see you!"

I am lost, she mumbled. I cannot be found.

He entered the living room and at first glance all he could see, in the ghastly light of the projector, was celluloid; clips and clips of celluloid snaking, curling one over the other, all over the coffee table, all over the floor.

"Edna?" he cried.

He bent over to turn off the machine, and it was there—in the darkest dark, right under that beam of light—that he stumbled over her. He brushed away the celluloid and, guided by nothing more than a sense of touch, passed a hand over her forehead, her eyelid, her ear, trying to piece together how she looked, and what had happened here.

"Wake up, babe," he whispered.

Her breathing was barely audible. He took a guess—by the grip of her fingers over her nose, and the subtle movement of her cheeks—that she was hiding a smile. Was it a game? Was she toying with him? He went down on all four, hanging over her, and could not believe his eyes. He must have been blinded, a second ago, by the glare. What he saw was unlikely. It was, perhaps, an illusion; a false sense of motion.

"Stop it, Edna," he shook her. "Wake up already!"

In her sleep she gave a faint cry. He rocked her, much gentler now, much more tenderly. Normally, after a long absence, it would take a bit of pampering for her to warm up to him—but so far, she seemed to remain cold. If he did not know any better, he would say she was under a spell.

She would not wake up. She was lost. Lost to him. The closer he came, the farther away she shrank. Trying to deny a sense of fear—for what was he fearing, really?—he considered whether or not he should give her a kiss.

"Can you hear me? Edna, can you hear me?"

Why was she so tightlipped? Look: She clasped a hand over her mouth as if her tongue had been bitten. The fingers were trembling, too. He took out a handkerchief and wiped them, for they were moist. There... There. To his astonishment, he sensed it again: Ever so slightly, that movement, still.

He wiped her chin. At once she froze, as if it was something forbidden, a pleasure she was hiding.

Ethan called her name again, this time in a soft, cooing sound, trying to pacify her. He whispered sweet nothings in her ear, raised her head to his lips, and gave it a quick peck. She uttered something: A vague, muffled moan with no words. It reminded him of the little sounds she would make in bed. He cradled her in his arms, tried playing with her fingers—but she fell back, away from him, pushed his hand away and, lost in her dream, went back to sucking her thumb.

And Then She Left Him

Uvi Poznansky, 2010

A nd then she left him.

He looks at the line. It is written in blue ink, pressed into the sheet of paper—vigorously here, faintly there—with his usual stroke, a stroke that drives through the spikes and valleys in the shapes of the letters at a steady slant. The line reaches the margin, where it is punctuated, unexpectedly, by a red stain.

Blotting it is bound to leave fingerprints, and so Mr. Schriber decides to leave it alone. He lifts the paper by its corner—and a drop bleeds down; he lays it down on the desk—and the stain goes on spreading. Going back to his writing, he applies too much pressure on the pen—and the pointed nib digs into the paper. Taking a deep breath, he tries to compose himself. The pen is his weapon. The simple act of pulling it over the soft, white surface has never failed to calm him down. Letter by letter, mark by mark, it will soon draw him into a different state of mind.

In this state, an alternative universe awaits him, a universe that exists in his mind, with details roughed out from memory or from imagination. This is his escape: A place faraway from the wild, maddening affairs of everyday life. Once there, Mr. Schriber will take control of his thoughts. He will be able, at last, to leave her behind.

He will populate this place with invented characters. Right now they are still a bit sketchy, nothing more than stick figures: A woman, and a man who loves her. He, the writer, will dictate their actions. He will choose when to reveal himself, giving them his emotions: Simple moments of joy, the intricacies of pain. At other times he will choose to mask himself, becoming that which he is not:

A woman, a man who loves her. In this place, he is God. He is the writer. He has control.

And then she left him.

These words are so painful to him, so penetrating, they feel like a pin through the core, a pin that fixes him in position, as if he were a dying butterfly. What other words are there? How else can his story start? Finding the right expression is always a fight: The writer in him wages battle against the editor; one is bold, the other—doubtful. They struggle inside him for control of his pen; one—to write, the other—to cross out.

Mr. Schriber reflects upon his writing method. In his mind, it is best to skip any introductions and open, quite abruptly, from the middle of things. There may have been some events in the past, events leading you up to that first sentence—but he, the writer, allows you just a sense of them, a sense vague enough just to come closer and listen.

Beginnings, he tells himself, are cheap. They come to him every morning by the dozen; and as easily as they come, he finds himself compelled to discard them. Too bad about the trees. Most of them have been sacrificed for nothing, for the pulp upon which he attempts to write his first, second and third drafts. His waste basket is already overflowing with crumpled beginnings.

An ending, on the other hand, is precious. It comes rarely, sometimes in a dream. He has to jot it down quickly, before it evaporates. A good ending allows the tale to linger in your mind, well beyond the last sound of the last sentence. It invites the words, utterances and expressions, the little fragments that float there nebulously, over his head, to come to him. Once captured, they will flow out of his pen. Only then will he pour himself out. But right now —without an end— Mr. Schriber is stuck.

For she was his muse.

The sad part, he wants to write, is not the fact that she left him. Nor is it the fact that she left him abruptly, after thirty-some years of marriage. At the time, it had taken him completely by surprise, for he adored her, wanted her all for himself, showered her with gifts, lavished money on her, took her abroad on expensive voyages and, being a good provider, insisted she should stay home, and forget about finding a job.

Her beauty had been diminished by time—but Mr. Schriber was blind to her puffy flesh, which she massaged morning and evening; blind to her thinning hair, which she teased up and curled constantly. What he saw was her eyes. There was a flash in them, a green flash that seared him and left a burn mark, especially when he caught her looking at him.

But most of the time she evaded him; which made her, in his eyes, even more alluring. He was consumed with jealousy when other men as much as laid eyes on her.

And then she left him.

He asked himself over and over, Why? How did he deserve it?

The kitchen table, bought in a garage sale long ago, when he was a young student, a couple of French landscape paintings, bought on the first morning of their honeymoon, and the festive set of china, which he bought her just last month, to celebrate their anniversary, were all carried off to her new place: An apartment his wife rented right around the corner. And so, his ability to dictate actions, either as a writer or as a husband, turned out to be nothing but fiction.

There was nothing real in it, nothing to which he could hang on. She abandoned him. Mr. Schriber was left there alone sitting at his desk, staring blankly out of his window, hoping; counting the seconds, the minutes until her return.

Now that, he thinks, is the saddest part of all. He wants to write about it, but cannot...

His hand trembles. Forgiveness is not in his character. He remembers threatening to divorce her, to take a new wife—but both of them knew these threats to be empty. So he threw himself feverishly into writing:

First, a story about handing Halloween candy to some kids, which —strangely enough—landed him in bed with the mother. Next, a story about attending a wedding ceremony, which landed him in bed with the bride. Then, a story about planning a Bar-Mitzva event, which landed him in bed with the Rebbitzin. Somehow, every female character he wrote ended up sharing these brief, outrageous adventures in his bed. The duller his life—the more uplifting became those hot, imagined quickies.

Meanwhile, his wife stayed estranged from him. Estranged—yet close. Close enough to keep an eye on him, and never let him go. How, then, could he recover? At every chance meeting, when he saw her walking on the other side of the street, she hinted that she might be coming back, perhaps tomorrow, perhaps next week.

Mr. Schriber wonders: Why did she say that? To quell his feelings —or to ignite them anew? There was no way to know for sure—but oh, how desperately he needed to believe! After a sleepless night he would call her, overcome by desire, as if he were a teenage boy. He yearned to lay his head in her bosom and cry, cry for the mistakes, the time lost, the missed opportunities.

As a writer he found a story with a happy ending to be boring—but now he hoped he yearned for one. He wished he could say, Let me tell you how things will turn out. But there was a lump in his throat; and so, when she picked up the phone he fell silent. Even so, she must have known how lonely he was, how much he wanted her back.

Her voice was distant, even cold at times. No, she insisted, there was no one else in her life. No one but him.

This month, however, she was too busy to talk, having been hired, just the other day, as a receptionist. There was, she said, too much pressure right now at work.

Then with a slam, she dropped the receiver at the other end. So well he remembers the sound of it. It must have been accidental. She could not feel that angry, that mad at him as to have done it on purpose.

At this point Mr. Schriber changes the period to a comma, hesitates, then adds a sentence: *She left him, saying she could only be his.*

As soon as he lifts up his hand, 'be his' gets absorbed, and sinks into the stain. He crosses out that entire sentence, and stares at what is left. Not much. He finds himself stumped. There is no flow to his story. The paper is still rustling there, under the shadow of his pen.

Thinking about his characters—a woman, a man—he scribbles a few notes to himself: Is the man too jealous? Does she hate him? Is she uneasy, for some reason? He drifts off for a while, then reads his notes again, aloud this time—but somehow they make no sense to him.

How can a woman feel uneasy, constricted by attention, even by jealousy? This is unbelievable! Unreal, really! He is a better writer than that! Isn't jealousy a sort of compliment, the highest, most sincere compliment a man can offer? His wife should be happy, she should be flattered that he loves her so much, so deeply!

Last night, he recalls, was again a restless one. He tossed off the blankets and got up in the dark, cursing himself, cursing her. When daylight finally broke in, it seemed to kick things off in the same manner as any other old day. The same words—he can still hear an echo of them—came stammering out of his mouth.

Secrets and lies, lies and deception!

She was driving him mad! He could not go on like this, trying to trust her, doing his best to suspend disbelief. This was his life—not some fiction! There was no patience, no time to pretend any longer.

For the sake of his sanity, he had to find out the truth. She could be his, only his—but was she?

Mr. Schriber knew the address of her office, having followed her there a few days earlier. He buttoned his shirt, placed the cover on the pen and stuck it in the shirt pocket. Then he dashed out the door. Walking at a brisk pace, he reached the intersection. There he halted at the red light, flanked on each side by men, tense young men in grey suits, who checked their watches every so often. This edginess, he decided, would be of use to him in fleshing out his characters. A woman; a man, waiting.

The man was still only a figure in his mind, a stick figure bracing itself for the most dramatic day of the tale of its life. Was the woman cheating on him? Would he kill her—or, perhaps, himself? The stick figure, like these jumpy men around him, could be coming to a stop; waiting at a red light, and checking its watch nervously.

Without even knowing how he got there, Mr. Schriber found himself standing in front of her office building. The glass doors swung open before him, giving him a glimpse of a small window directly across from him, on the back wall of the lobby. Reflected in the windowpane was a slender woman. She was dressed in a low-cut, blue blouse. From a distance, it looked like a mark of indigo ink. He saw the big hairdo and suddenly recognized his wife.

At once he turned around and went out. His heart pounding, he found a dirt path around the building, located that window and cowered underneath the ledge. The bushes at his back were prickly, so he could not allow himself to lean against them. His feet dug themselves into a hole.

From time to time he straightened his back, took a quick peep at her through the window, and hunkered down again.

Some insect fluttered away; perhaps a butterfly. Something that felt like a worm crawled around his sock and into his pants. The sun kept rising. He rose, glanced inside and ducked, only to rise, glance and duck, over and again. After an hour of this spying routine, Mr. Schriber was wet with sweat. His knees swelled, and his leg muscles started to burn under him—but he was bent on his task. He pulled his pen out of the shirt pocket, perhaps with a vague intention of taking notes. Clearly, the information he was gathering became more and more troubling:

First, a few people lined up in front of her. Five minutes later she was alone, leafing through some paperwork. Next he noticed a man, an incredibly tall man with broad shoulders, dressed in a business suit. The man approached her. Five minutes later, they were still chatting. From a distance, the conversation seemed to be overly friendly; there was too much warmth, too much familiarity between the two of them. Then Mr. Schriber caught his wife swaying her hips in a bold, flirtatious manner and alas, smiling.

He had to hide a little longer this time, suspecting that someone on the inside might have spotted his head, bobbing up and down, up and down over the windowsill.

By now it must have been noontime. Drenched in sweat, he glanced over his shoulder at the thorny branches surrounding him; and suddenly the shame, the humiliation of where he found himself and what he was doing caught up to him. No woman was worth it; was she?

He rose to his feet with a sigh, prepared to give up and go home, and then caught a sound, the sound of snapping branches coming from behind. Mr. Schriber turned around when—out of nowhere—a heavy fist pounded him square on his chin, making him sway back and forth until finally, losing his balance. The only thing that cushioned his fall was the prickly brush behind him.

Standing victoriously over him, a big halo of sunshine crowning his head, was that man, the tall man he has spotted earlier. His shoulders seemed even broader at this close range. Without a single word, he stepped forth even closer and—without a warning—set his foot down, directly on top of Mr. Schriber's shoulder.

Meanwhile, a head appeared at the window above him. "What happened?" cried Mr. Schriber's wife. "What are you doing down there? You stalking me?"

Lying there helpless, flat on his back, exposed to her scrutiny, Mr. Schriber felt his face turning red. Scolded by the heat of the sun and by the green flame in her eyes, he bit his lips. There was no way, no reasonable way to answer, which—quite inevitably—ignited his anger. And so, armed with nothing more than a pen, he thrust out his hand, aiming straight up at the man who attacked him.

His weapon rose in the air, flipping reflections in the sunlight. It went spinning, rising higher and higher in its flight toward the attacker, who raised his hand, attempting to snatch the thing, catch it —

But then, the man must have lost his footing on the ground, for he came down heavily, snapping at branches, even breaking some of them along the way. The only thing that cushioned his fall was none other than Mr. Schriber, who found himself all of a sudden pinned down, and utterly short of breath. Nonetheless he managed a sharp, shrill cry, and raised his eyes to heaven.

Which was where the pen took a turn in its flight. It arched—ever so slowly—over the frame of the window, and missed his wife's head by no more than a hair. She parted her painted lips; her smile was tinged, he noted, tinged with revenge.

She held out her hand, waiting calmly for the thing to reach her. Having clasped it, she started dangling the pen playfully, leaning over the two men lying there, one on top of the other. A thought flashed in Mr. Schriber mind: Whom would she choose? Would it be him? Does she still love him? Does she hate—

The pointed nib gave a steely glint.

The last thing he saw, just before passing out, was her eyes. At that instant, he thought he saw a flash of insanity. She winked at him, and he yearned for her, he could sense the beating of her heart, the danger. Then, with a swift motion, she took aim...

How long has he stayed there? Mr. Schriber has no idea; it could have been seconds or hours. He cannot recall how he managed to free himself from the weight of the man on top, or even if there was such as weight at all. Nor can he remember the way back, how he carried himself back home.

But somehow his confusion starts to clear up. Now he knows, deep inside, how she must have felt all these years. Confined. Caged. He has a sudden sense of her anguish. No longer does he wonder why, why she would wish to hurt him. To his surprise, he finds himself coming, at long last, to accept her way of looking at things. He embraces what she has been giving him. He takes it in, her hate.

Is it too late for him? Too late to turn a new page? Can he hold on, just long enough to try, try to tell her he is sorry? At this point Mr. Schriber grips the arms of the chair and with great effort, lifts himself into it. Then he leans over his desk, feeling tired, and older than he ever felt before. From time to time he presses one hand to his temple, where a sharp pain shoots through him. His other hand clutches the weapon: his pen.

He can tell, there is not much time. The ending has come to him at long last; and so the battle between the writer in him and the editor, the battle that has been waged inside his mind, turns easy all of a sudden, and the triumph—joyous.

The pain recedes, and now he pours his heart out, filling one sheet of paper after another with his bold, fluid stroke, a stroke that drives through the spikes and valleys in the shapes of the letters, at a steady slant. In this landscape of blue ink, he writes without stopping, without editing or crossing anything out. He feels the urge. Time is running out.

Then Mr. Schriber lays his head on the wooden surface of the desk. Time to give up control. Time to give up... So he listens to the pen rolling softly away from his fingers, farther and farther out of reach, until there is nothing there, nothing but silence. He lets his eyes fall shut and at long last, falls asleep.

In his dream he views this last sheet of paper. Its texture, seen at an extremely close range, is that of crushed, flattened pulp. He notes each and every fiber. Yes, he imagines can tell them apart by the subtle changes in direction, and in the shades of their whiteness. The paper carries a faint but indelible imprint, a stain that has, by now, seeped through the entire stack. But if you passed a finger over it, it would feel dry to the touch.

At this moment the stain seems to have changed colors; it has turned dark brown, even inky in places. And here, close to the edge you could find a fingerprint. This is the writer's signature, this and no other, because sleep came abruptly, before he had time to spell out his name. And there—scribbled with a strained gesture, directly above this signature—are these last words:

She said, Time to go. He asked her forgiveness, and then she left him.

31

Blade

Uvi Poznansky, 2004[2]

I have no will. I have no curiosity. Of its own, my finger is passing with barely a touch along the blade until suddenly, catching on a spot, it halts. Rust, perhaps. I raise my hand over to the light, careful not to tighten my hold over the thing. A cold shine can be seen in intervals, shooting up and down between my fingers along the metallic handle. I can sense the edge.

I can see my wrist, a vein twisting through it with a hard pulse. I can see the delicate lines, guessing their way across the skin. How frail is life. Better close your eyes. Close your eyes, I say. Do it.

I close my eyes and with a light, effortless relief, my thoughts are lifted, flying away from the moment. They are lifted, turning over the edge, cutting up and away, heading for a far, far time in the past.

I have no will. I have no curiosity.

What now, I ask. What if I have no blood. What if I am no longer here.

---

[2] These words, jotted down in Uvi's diary, found their way into her novel, *Apart from Love*. There, they are spoken in Ben's voice.

Even One Mark

Uvi Poznansky, 2010

She wanted to write about her life; but looking at the empty page, the top one in a stack that laid there in her lap, she found the idea of writing intimidating. If she were to put down even one letter—even one mark—it would mar the purity of the page, and replace it irrevocably with clutter.

She was afraid, so afraid now, of clutter.

Lately she found it more and more difficult to follow the thread of her thought. She was lost, lost in her own labyrinth. Fragments of ideas floated dreamily across her mind, stumbled by foreign-sounding words and interrupted, from time to time, by images of faded faces, images that were yellowing and crumpled around the edges like old photographs.

How much longer could she pretend to be holding it together?

The air was no longer still. A sudden gust of wind ruffled through the pages. Soon the evening breeze would come passing through. She could see the bony white knuckles as she clutched at the pen. She wanted to write about her life, and tried to remember who she was, to whom she was writing, and for what purpose.

It would have been so much easier to write from a point of view other than herself. Perhaps the point of view of some inanimate object. A doorknob. It would be simple to pretend to be—no, to become one. The notion of being a doorknob—of it seeing her as she was, surrounded by her children, it seeing each one of her children as they grew up, crossing the threshold, coming in and out over the course of a lifetime—that notion somehow appealed to her.

At first, she imagined, the doorknob would reflect, with its shiny distortion, the image of her youth. It would feel her hand—warm and firm, in those days—as she pushed the door open, letting the children out to play, and later calling them back in for lunch, after which she would clear the table, mop the floor, wash the dishes and wipe them dry. She would even wipe the doorknob. It felt polished and happy.

In the course of time, when the children left home, and especially when they moved oversees and took the grandchildren with them, the doorknob would lose its smoothness. It would become uneven, even cloudy; she could no longer trust the distortion it offered. Maybe things never really happened the way it mirrored them.

Now she could get a narrow glimpse of the sunset. The door was ajar, twisting in the cold air. After a while, its hinges started to creak. She retreated to her kitchen, although there was no one there anymore for whom she could cook. For a long time she listened to the leaves blowing across the street, out there in the distance where children could be heard laughing. She listened to the door creaking in the wind, and waited patiently for a sign, a note, a word of some sort; kept on waiting until—with one croak—the door closed.

She locked herself in and started writing letters, some of which were never sent, for fear of revealing too much of her loneliness. Other letters she embellished along the margins, with a hand heavy with years but with the manner of a schoolgirl: She embellished them with pink flowers and long sequences of x's and o's for kisses and hugs, and then she sent them to that foreign sounding address, so that her grandchildren, who rarely came to visit, would know she loved them.

How would a doorknob feel to be barely touched, its latch rarely released, the lock always bolted shut? How would it feel to be in the grip of rust?

She glanced at the doorknob. Would it retain a memory of her touch, even when she is gone? Would it keep, in its own transparent ways and despite all that polishing, the layers upon layers of all their fingerprints?

She wanted to write about her life, and tried to remember who she was, to whom she was writing, and for what purpose; but if she were to put down even one letter—even one mark—all her love, all her loneliness, and all that bitter disappointment that this was all life had to offer in the end, would come rushing out, and nothing in the world could hold her together any more.

So without looking at the empty page, without embellishing the margins with pink flowers, and without long sequences of x's and o's for kisses and hugs, she marked one single, long line, as if writing with her trembling hand the whole length of the story of her life. Then, with a sense of finality, she crossed it. An X.

The wind whipped the pages out of her lap. They flew around her, some settling to the ground, some flipping higher, flapping into a big clutter in the air, then floating dreamily away across the landscape. In years past she would get up, catch them one by one and stack them back, with a strict attention to order; but now she didn't care anymore. For a moment she thought she could see that page, the one she had marked X with a trembling hand. There it was, a white glimmer soaring out of reach above her in the wind. And then, in one puff, it was over.

Somewhere inside, a doorknob broke. A door flew open.

Don't Open Your Eyes

Uvi Poznansky, 2004

Don't open your eyes
   Try not to see

Things are no longer

Where things ought to be

That voice—is it her?

Behind a closed door

She calls you a stranger

Your mother no more

Breathe through the moment

Turn, turn your eyes

The past you imagined

Was all lies, lies, lies

Things are no longer

Where things ought to be

Who is this stranger

Is it still me?

This Tissue Is Me

Uvi Poznansky, 2012[3]

S himmering luster, let me try, let me reach you

Layers beyond layers of red, all aglow

With trembling fingers I touch... Flimsy tissue

It comes down upon me, folding high into low

I dance with abandon, with no inhibition,

Entangled in fabric, I can no longer flee

Can't breathe, for now I can sense the strange fusion

Now I know: this tissue is me—

---

[3] This poem was inspired by Uvi's artwork, a triptych of oil paintings called *Entangled*. The cover image of the novel *Apart from Love* also originated from the same triptych.

Be Still, A Poet's Heart

Uvi Poznansky, 2012

Be still, poet's heart, this moment is rare
Stop this hammering, why would you dare
To set up a challenge, to write your own fate
Be still and accept, perhaps it's too late

Unlucky the number, unlucky the day
Still, welcome the future, come what may
Set yourself free, apart from love
Change whatever was decreed from above

Sing out a ballad of passion and hate
Sing it out as you drown, and ignore that date
Someone may notice, may listen out there
So quicken the pounding, sing out with a flair

The flood is abating, release the dove
Pray to find yourself a part of love

A Diamond Short, A Decade Late

Uvi Poznansky, 2007

A diamond short, a decade late
I come to stand outside your gate

Unlock and open, let me in

Forgive me, love; what is my sin?

I fled from you across the land

But now I ask you for your hand

A decade late, a diamond short

I can't imagine why you snort

My limbs are frail, my breath is cold

I must admit I may look old

I fall, I kneel, why—I implore

You are the woman I adore

I feel so weak, I feel so brittle

Don't touch! I may be impotent a little

You loved me once—or so I thought

Stop! Take your fingers off my throat—

Snarl

Uvi Poznansky, 2014

At first I snarl, snaking

In the dirt around your foot,

I wish to shoot up, lifting

My body from the soot

I coil up, all around you

Weaving shadows into your light

Your white, now brushed with my blue

Is no longer pure--not quite--

And as I reach, your neck to clutch

And lean in with a hiss

Your head floats off, now out of touch

So far out of my kiss

How can I reach your temple?

I can't, now I know

You are so high, so gentle

You tremble in the flow...

Plucked Porcupine

Uvi Poznansky, 2014

I miss the swish of grass and clover

The crunch of twigs, no pangs, no hunger,

That place is far--I must not pine--

For a poor, plucked porcupine

I watch out for the angry poet

I stumble back, too late to exit,

She glares at me, at these sharp spines

Her ink has spilled, so here she whines

I hate, I hate to wish her ill

She writes this poem with my quill

Dust

Uvi Poznansky, 2014

From dust you gather me

I beg you on my knee

Look away—imagine me,

The way I used to be

Now shadows spread upon me

Stain by stain

I shiver. Touch me, heal me

Make me whole again

I see him in my mind

He moves, he stirs tonight

But when I come to him,

Our limbs entwined

That arm wraps around me

It holds me and controls me—

Can we take flight?

In darkness take a leap

For trust is blind

Imagine me: I'll lift you,

Caress you and possess you

Imagine us:

In passion and in sweep

Our limbs entwined

Pressed against that ribcage

Where not a breath escapes

Not a sigh of sorrow,

Not a cry of rage

How can I bear his silence

When shadows grow immense—

If shadows peel and lift away

If ever you break free

From my embrace

If you catch sight of me

In light of day—

Go... Leave me here,

My grace,

In my debris—

In my dream I'm soaring

Amidst a flap of wings

My heart so light,

So happy,

Forgetting him, ignoring

That arm

Wrapped around me,

How heavily it clings

Go!

My spirit crushed and humble

No feeling left, no lust

Abandoned here To crumble…

Not strong enough to blow

These fading marks of footfalls,

Your footfalls, off my dust…

I will not let you blur

These traces in my mind

Of the way we were

Our limbs entwined

I miss you, still resist you,

Forgive me, for I must

Gather you so gently

From the dust.

Tango

Uvi Poznansky, 2023

No more idle time and no more blues!

I'll curl up my mustache, put on dancing shoes

I need someone — you? — whose heart I can steal

For Heaven's sake, don't make me kneel

        I dabbed some perfume just under my ear

        As soon as I laid eyes on you, dear

        You move with panache, with such elegant flair

        I adore your bald spot, your dwindling hair

Yes, I think of myself as a dashing young man

No surprise you came over as the music began

My aftershave is intoxicating, I am in such bliss

As I lean over, shall I give you a kiss?

        I painted my lips, put a rose in my hair

        My bosom is plump, my arms are bare,

        As I cling to you — what a tall gentleman! —

        Can you hear my heart? Hold me tight if you can

I sway on my feet, then leap into the air

Come tango with me—if only you dare

Hang on my arm, let me lead step by step

Oh my darling, now your weight I must shlep

Eyes Fallen Shut

Uvi Poznansky, 2024

If my eyes fall shut, there's no darkness around me

Walls tumble away… I'm not locked in a box

If my ears turn deaf, there's no suffering. I'm free

Of this incessant ticking of silenced blank clocks

Cursed to wait, wait, wait still longer to dart

When someone out there releases a grip

Now I sense a slight spin… A hinge, stirring… A start

As my lid cranks, cracks, creaks open, out I slip

Ready or not, here I come… What a loud Pop!

Do I strike fear? Make your heart freeze?

Held up ever-so-briefly, how soon shall I drop

Back into oblivion, back into a squeeze?

Till I'm found again, forgotten, confined

I'll be dreaming of you, your eyes fallen shut

Zeev Kachel

(Blue Wolf)

Poems

Translated from Hebrew by
Uvi Poznansky

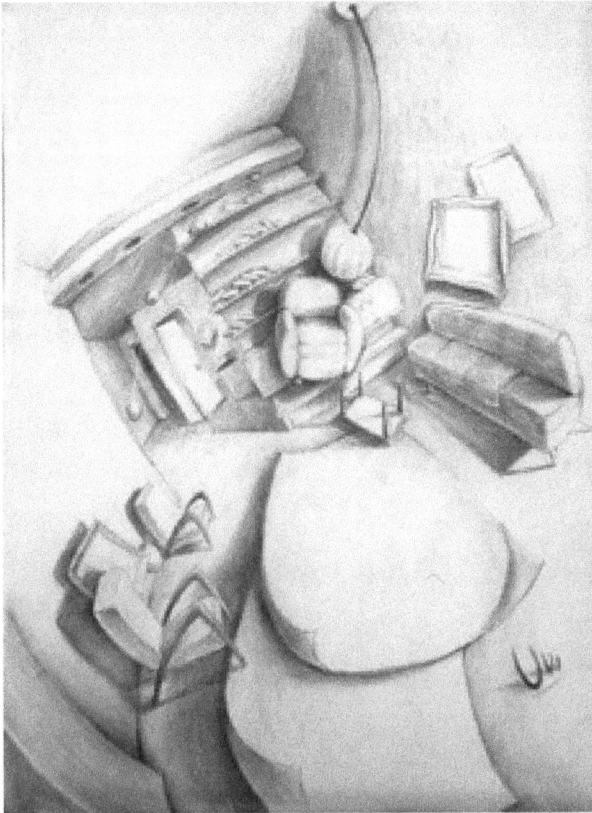

Reparations

Zeev Kachel, 1966

Y ou're asking me to put here in writing, once more,
All that I lost, my esteemed counselor?
To list in detail, then describe and refine
And bring two witnesses tomorrow to sign?

My father's gold watch—I could just hear the sound
Had three lids that were shining
Reflected in it I could see us, standing around
All faces aglow and rejoicing.

The watch also had a heavy gold chain
Coiled twice over, over his vein
The tips of its hands gave a hint of a spark
Shooting green glow, right into the dark

It ticked, counting years for each girl and boy
Marking seasons, holidays, morning and night
I remember Sabbath candles flickering with joy
Sparkling brightly, like starlight.

You're asking me to record, on paper to pour

All that I lost, my esteemed counselor?

There was an old synagogue my grandpa had built

Burning scrolls, flying ash, dying spirit

Ancient Torah aflame, letters lifting, all gilt

Thou shall not kill, shall not steal, shall not covet

And there was my sister: delicate, tender

In her eyes I remember a twinkle

Her name was Batia, my beloved little sister

She grew up—and then—it was simple:

She grew up and married, and gave birth to a son

With a blue glint in his eyes, and a dimple

Blond hair, just like a pure 'Aryan'—

The murderers, they threw him right into the Nile

There were aunts, and uncles, boys and girls in our midst

The murderers decreed: they should not exist

You're asking me to record, on paper to pour

All that I lost, my esteemed counselor?

I demand to return, reopen that door

Find parents and sister, each girl and boy

Home

Back there in that synagogue, with that spirit of yore

Sabbath candles aflame, father's voice filled with joy.

It's not property I ask for, not mere pieces of land—

Hebrew school, friends around, all of us in one band

With hope that inspired to survive, to withstand.

Bring the murderers to trial, that is all I demand.

You will not understand; it's of no great import—

I demand that which had been cut short.

We Were Born in Darkness

Zeev Kachel, 1988

We were born in darkness, crying a fit

And like grains of sand, countless stars came up, lit,

We wanted to turn back to the warm womb

Instead we were wrapped by chill and by gloom

Born in darkness, we labored so hard

To find our way in this universe

We were greeted by its hug, its cruelty, its curse

Its predators' jaws... We're forced to traverse.

Ma, why did you fool me, what was it for,

When you sang me a lullaby, not a song of war?

Oh why did you hide the fateful truth from me

We were born in darkness, our life—not to be?

After You're Gone

Zeev Kachel

Somewhere at night a string sings out
All's dark, silent, filled with doubt
I'm alone, and you?
Out there, in the cold, a string sings out

Forgive me ma, that under your wing
A poet grew, only to sing
Forgive me ma, I knew no way but run
I was a defiant son!

In your life I sang you no songs, but now I miss—
Forgive me ma, that I wiped off your kiss
Which you gave me, thinking I were asleep...
Now, after you're gone, I confess and I weep

I loved no one like you!
After you were gone, I knew
I had travelled to a place so alien, so cold
How bitter it had felt, to you I never told.

How you waited to receive a word from me, a letter,

How I missed you! Only now I know better

No longer am I ashamed to say, to try:

Forgive me ma, now at last I am allowed to cry.

Childhood Years

Zeev Kachel

C hildhood years, a realm of dreams and charms
How fast you petered out, forever lost to me
How fast you hurtled away, without a harness
Race on, *Troika*, bells ringing with such jubilee

How fast it all passed away forever,
Galloped away, as if it never was:
But somewhere in the mist, with such a quiet measure
Someone sings for me without a pause

Only yesterday we threw each other snowballs
Only yesterday we played games of pretend,
Only yesterday we swam there, right across the creek
And told each other stories, of which I won't speak

Around us is a boundless, snowy marvel
And you, my little sister, pressed against my heart
Wail of wolves, and ma beside us, fearful
Horses trotting, trotting... Our childhood, cut short

In the distance, you seem to spot a shelter

But all I see is an endless universe

Come on, *Troika*!⁴ Snow sparkles on your lashes

Lets charge to the horizon, let us chart our course!

---

⁴ *Troika* is a sled or carriage drawn by three horses harnessed side-by-side, iconic symbol of Russia

My Teachers

Zeev Kachel, 1991

My first art teacher was the chill

The chill that painted forests and cities

Across my window pane, with icicles and frost

In Poland, she whose hate scorched Jews, and wished us ill

She who set my heart burning to sail to a new coast

My second teacher was time

Time that tipped my hair with silver over and again

Time that whitened my mustache, even in my prime

Time like a wolf's wail, flowing in my vein

My third teacher was the dream

The dream that I nurtured from the day I was born

In an era of storms that flared up with a scream

The dream that grew in me, to which I was sworn

They punished me harshly with their rods

Instilled joy of creation within my crumbling walls.

Fall

Zeev Kachel

L eaves are falling
And an Autumn wind is blowing.

I'm alone.

Ringing in my ear

Is it you, who's thinking about me?

The walls close in upon me, like a prison.

I dreamt a dream that I'm still a child,

Here's home.

In a minute the door will open

Letting in my parents, my sister.

I'm foolishly beguiled!

They were all swept off by a gust, into the wild

I'm alone

No longer a child.

Memory

Zeev Kachel, 1987

When the past becomes your present
And follows you everywhere
Like a hunting dog, it's so intent
Then memory becomes despair

Memory, in a sudden spell
Then becomes your daily routine
Reality turns into hell
A crazy race to the unseen

You set your ladder on a ripple
No wonder that you fell, you cripple

Every Day I Tear A Leaf

Zeev Kachel, 1964

E very day I tear a leaf
From my calendar, blanched by the sun

Here's spring... It is so brief

Leaves now falling, one by one...

Once more it's spring, the fragrance's sweet

And blossom spreads again, again

With graying hair, there in the street

I sit: a lonely, crestfallen man

Do you remember: a student's room

With a single narrow iron bed

That eve of golden summer bloom

We fried potatoes, words unsaid

The plates we set down on the floor

And filled our glass with cheap, warm wine

Between our kisses, love we swore...

For that lost moment, how I pine!

A star came on, peeking in

Out of the depth of a strange, dark night

The entire world was here within

A serenade of love, delight

She and I

Zeev Kachel

I 'm dying to sleep, but oh
She's eager to get going
All because of a little window
And tempers that are blowing

I close it gingerly
So she demands it open
I want to sleep, but woefully
She'll shake it till it's broken

By nature she's outgoing
I'm quiet, her willing complement
She's totally inconsistent
Consistently my opposite

She craves parties, more and more
While a lone wolf am I
Her desire—a burly sailor
While a dreamy poet I

She longs for flowers

And I—for chocolate

She wants adventure at all hours

While I dream only 'bout my ballad

I want the window closed

And she prefers it open

She hates that I have snored

In concerts, and never woken

She wants to learn to drive

While I can die of fright

The drive is easier to survive

When in the back we're hugging tight

She deserves dresses galore

And a burning passion

Yet I have only two loves, no more:

My homeland and my nation

Two loves that I adore

Are me, and you with a bouquet

And one more

The Sabbath day.

Lie to Me

Zeev Kachel, 1975

L ie to me, it's your way to give
     Lie well, and I will trust you

The only one able to forgive

Is my heart, so true

Lie and I will trust you

Go ahead, lie well

'Cause joy's dead, it's all but through

Once the pain I quell

Then we'll raise an empty glass,

Each one of us alone, to toast

A version of truth, which now we pass

As our life, almost.

I Forgive You Everything

Zeev Kachel, 1987

I forgive you everything—
     Your nearly honest acting,

Your pretense, the imitation of faithfulness

Abuse of trust, exposing me to laughter

The loneliness, into which you thrust me,

     The whispers all around

The weeping, deep inside me, the weeping with no sound.

    Just tell me why

Did I deserve it.

Now all is known. It's finally in the open.

Your timing is good,

    Your planning—perfect!

I forgive you everything: The agony, sorrow too,

The only thing I care about is the pain that I caused you.

Stinging flies, come closer, taste my blood

I'll figure for myself how to sink into the mud

Don't be a Judge

Zeev Kachel, 1988

D on't be a judge before you've been roughed up
Don't be soft!

I despise politeness

From this battle, I'm not going to escape.

Survived so far. Will not give an inch. I cuss

Until a change takes shape

Let a whip rule between us.

Weep, My Heart

Zeev Kachel, 1988

Weep, my heart, with not a tear

In the dark, in secret

Let no one see me, for I fear

Their scheme, their plot, their threat

Let the traitors never see me

Those who mock me now

Let them not pretend to save me

That I won't allow

Behind my back, those gossipmongers

I sense them point at me

The fools, I hear them in large numbers

Laughing at my calamity

Not to Think

Zeev Kachel, 1988

T he place has sunk in darkness, almost dead
   One light's out there, flickering in that window
You're here across the bed, eagle spread
She out there, in her home, waiting for you
Strange, too!
You're lying here, and on your head—the pillow.

In your brain, thoughts keep turning, grinding
How to lift the darkness?
How not to think?
Like flesh off a prey, you at yourself keep tearing
If only you could love again, again you could caress—

I'm Not Sorry

Zeev Kachel, 1988

I 'm not sorry for the hours that I wasted
Suspended in my dreams and idle thought
I'm not sorry for the days I ruined
The only thing I care about is the luster I did blot

I care that that's the way our lives are going
In power games, for which we'll pay the price,
I ache, because of our misunderstanding
Because that which is between us turned hard as ice

I care nothing for the roses that have withered
Over their fleeting fragrance I will shed no tears
What pains me now is the way I hurt you
And that if I ask forgiveness, no one hears

No way to settle this, to heal the cuts
In this world there's a price for everything
The echo of our steps is the witness left behind us
As the light that glowed upon us is already blackening.

Not One is Home

Zeev Kachel, 1987

T wo apartments I own—not one is home
 I have acquaintances, among whom I'm alone
And a laurel wreath, with thorns around my dome.
I've cast in the anchor
And yet, I'm far blown

My arrogance is buried, my stupidity too
I've climbed higher than my ladder would allow
Wrapped in a different garb I walked among you
But fell short of reaching heaven, somehow

I had a shock of hair, but now completely bald
My feathers have been plucked off, one by one
I built a nest, where now a *guest* I'm called
With the crowd I march away, undone

Your Advocate, Your Voice

Zeev Kachel, 1989

I 've been your advocate, your voice
Against my own allegations that be
You pulled sideways, or so I imagined; by choice
I'll blame no one else now but me.

Where's the hand for which I've been waiting
The hand of the one under a mask
My savior, for whom I've been praying
When would he execute me, I ask?

I bolted and chained every lock here
Thinking of the noose he would tie
So weary am I, suspended in fear
Dreading to live or to die.

My Girl of Innocence, from Time to Time

Zeev Kachel, 1990

Accept regards from a lonely wolf like me
Regards sent without a single word
At the end of the day, a cost dispute is but poverty,
Again here comes the Sabbath, and we are separate.

Four years have passed since the day you left home
And in the closet hangs a single dress,
It's nightfall. There sits the Prince of Verse
Surrounded by four walls, entirely alone.

What have you solved there?
        You too alone each evening
Facing that stupid TV, there you stare:
A cost dispute, like a double sword, is cutting
Inflicting injuries on either side.

A newborn wonders about our strange existence
And someone thinks, for what purpose was he born?

Home

Do you still remember our bouts of silence?

Descending here again comes Sabbath Queen, forlorn

Gone are those days of anger, of blind jealousy

And something inside me has vanished in its prime

If sadness has passed away, so soon will felicity

My girl of innocence, from time to time

My Ties Unhitched

Zeev Kachel, 1988

My ties unhitched, now I am glum.

A tad sad, to be neglected

Today I celebrated being lonesome

My joy was somewhat limited.

Sit here with me, and let us talk

Of what was gained, what lost, and why

Let us somehow try, take stock

You're confused, and so am I

Please tell me something more about you

The problems, the family

Of all your friends, who remained true

And who turned his back on your agony?

I'm so exhausted of the journey

I can muster no more strength

All this is claptrap, it's all but corny

Every kin—a stranger, at arm's length

I'm left to my own soul searching

Yet taking account I find so hard

I'd rather send my soldiers charging:

Load mud into the artillery; bombard!

Chiribim-chiribom, all's upside

What is left for me to try?

Life is but a suicide

Not even worth a single sigh.

We Met Here

Zeev Kachel

We met here for a fleeting moment
Bonded by a glance, which now is absent:
Again you're gone, again not here. Bereft
Of having you, alone I'm left

Somewhere There

Zeev Kachel

S omewhere there, are you too crouching in a corner
Recalling me to mind, your eye agleam?
Or have you forgotten me, in love no longer
Are you thinking now: that was but a dream

In My Dream I Hear

Zeev Kachel, 1989

I n my dream I hear your voice, the voice I lack

You're here beside me. You care for me, you've come back

And that deceitful shadow moved away, no longer black...

We're back together, just like in the past

The heart's aglow, no darkness, at long last—

Another Time

Zeev Kachel, 1988

A nother time, in another town
Faraway from here, on some other shore,

Like a memory you go down

Under a foreign sky that can't soar

Facing the sea I sit in darkness

Upon a single bench, there on the beach

And then, then I dream: perhaps happiness

Will again emerge from out of reach

Infinity, shine upon me... I beseech.

Never have the Days

Zeev Kachel, 1989

N ever have the days passed by so slowly
   Never has time crawled, ever so frightfully
The bad time, it stretches on, up to no end
The good time fleets, like lightning you can't wend.

And what shall we remember? Both times as yet
One day, perhaps, good and bad we'll regret

We Pass

Zeev Kachel

We pass by each other without speaking, dumbly

We look at each other—blindly

Loneliness crying out of our eyes

But we keep on, silently.

Each one of us carrying a load

Each one suffering, utterly slowed

Each one going on, down this road

See there, a couple just passed in embrace.

We used to walk this way, do you still remember?

You looked forward to my coming.

In the midst of spring blossom, here's the sorrow of fall.

And the recognition that it's all over.

Today, between us came a wall.

Now, never to return, life has all

But passed. That is fall.

No one to shake a hand, no one to give a nod.

You and me, through this isolation we plod.

It's fall: all flawed.

Glass Eyes

Zeev Kachel

We pass each other
As if strangers, in disguise
We look at each other
Out of glass eyes

We pass each other
Unable to hear
Our hearts crying out, brother!
Give a hand, come here!

Our ears blocked to hearing
And the heart—in a foreskin
Who was that? Just a trace of something
Not a human, not a kin

Please, do not fear me,
It's not your purse I want; please stay
Tomorrow is as empty
As yesterday

Among a bustling crowd I stare

Searching for just one friend,

And none is there.

Not one. A bitter end.

Here passes a 'replacement'

Casting a look. Again

Your prayers were in vain.

Not in Good Spirits

Zeev Kachel, 1988

T oday I am not in good spirits
Today I will laugh at myself,
Against me I will lay all my bets
And come face to face with myself

Today I'm sad, my heart beats
In vain will I search for a friend,
Today I will wander the streets
And into temptations descend.

Soon night will fall, it will blacken
My own hand I'll see only barely,
As always I'll go on, forsaken
Before long I shall no longer be

Will my friends talk of me with contempt
Will she listen? I am betrayed,
Will they pass me by and attempt
To evade me in the grand masquerade?

Crossroad

Zeev Kachel, 1990

At a crossroad here I stand
I kick the past, I kick it, and

I find my lodging somewhere near

I find that I am not quite here

I am not here, I am not there

Not awake, not asleep, unable to bear

And you, a dove, will fly away

Will not return come spring day

The blessed moments don't return

I've ruined everything, my life I spurn

The hours pass, here comes the night

The day is gone, are you alright?

I'm not alive, I am not dead

I kick the past, and on I tread.

No Need to Worry Anymore

Zeev Kachel, 1988

No need to worry anymore

It's all coming to an end

No need to rage anymore.

Silence's here, 'bout to descend.

Only the notes of the piano

Are trembling here, in the still

No need to sob anymore

It's a world of deceit

Weeping here is the mandolin

Wailing is the string

This evening's reward is the bitterness of night

I'll never understand why I'm fated to blight

A Different Man

Zeev Kachel, 1992

I 'm a different man today.
Not the one you know

You can come back

If you will.

I'm a different man today, without a hat I go

But in my heart—there's still.

I'm a different man.

Just the way you preferred

I fulfilled your wish

Wandering along your street without a word

Looking for you—in vain, in anguish.

I'm different today.

Not the man you left.

Not pressuring anyone—

The way you wanted me to be,

Just looking for you everywhere—

But you, a stranger, moving on

And after all—you have been wishing well for me

I am different—

Not the one you know

You can come back

Just confirm

I am different—

Not raging anymore

But in my heart—a worm.

I'm different today—

Refraining from correcting everything.

Silent, not a word

My journey at its end:

Time to go back, here I'm done…

I won't bother anyone.

Everything has Long Lost Its Weight

Zeev Kachel, 1988

Everything has long lost its weight:
Wife, and values, and stock
All that's left is a confused haze of fate
A night with no time and no clock

Left here is a pensive old man
Consumed by the waves, shelled, expelled
And also your dear memory, then
That suddenly sprouted and swelled

Should I Fall

Zeev Kachel, 1985

S hould I fall, stranger's hands will lift me,

Take me to a place, who knows where

Only celestial bodies from afar will follow me

And a garden bench will mourn me, lonely and bare.

A bench where I sat will be left there, behind

As orphaned as I am, down in the meadow

And the figure with whom I became one in my mind

Will not happen to pass by, nor take in the echo

Should I fall.

Now I Cry

Zeev Kachel, 1992

Now I cry but not with tears; inside
After long, long years
Of holding it
Now I cry
Out of a burst of pain
And howl in darkness out of loneliness
Now I give my pain its full release
With no shame, no stops. Dead hopeless

Tired. Tired of life
Tired of people
Of betrayals, of being double-crossed
I am tired.
The phone is silent.
No one calls anymore
The wall in front of me speaks, its language—hard
The phone is silent.
No one cares anymore
The only sound amidst the silence is writing in my mind.

When Life Becomes a Curse

Zeev Kachel, 1990

When life becomes a curse
Like a stone-mill you must heft
No one's here to ask for help
Not a single friend is left
Then your soul is bitter, cleft.

The children flew, one far, one distant...
Four walls, the home is vacant
How can you hug her, she is absent
No one left but memories
Then the heavy burden slaps
A man on the verge of his collapse.

Without a Compass

Zeev Kachel, 1974

A sad story about a happy man, a man who
Loved poems, women, and a calm core
A sad story that crashed against the cliff, crashed onto
A cold, indifferent shore

Hey, captain of our fates, let your hand be firm
Amidst the torque of time, amidst the murk
Navigate our ship through this night, this storm
Towards the light that beacons from the dark

Save us from the gulf deep here within us
And from a smile that bares sharp teeth
Give us strength to withstand our faults, our weakness
Against ourselves give us a shield, a sheath

Oh God! The sunrise comes upon us
But inside—still night, without a compass

The Wolf

Zeev Kachel, 1970

F ini la comédie! Adieu, dear friends!
  The spectators wipe their noses... I'm all yours!
Like a philosopher, the body now contends
With a damp grave, and worms, scores and scores

No wails, my friends, and no fake sympathy
Nothing do I want, no one do I miss
Please, no crocodile tears, and no fake eulogy,
In front of a silent grave, no praise, no hiss

The wolf, he's alone, once more.
Amongst the crowd of mourners
Here are the frog, the snake, the jackal I abhor
Pretty lizards, a worm in the corner,
And one blue wolf, so sore.

Let the sea under my headstone forever hum and spread,
Let the wind thrum, strum my mandolin
And let the moonlight gently kiss the forehead
That pondered love, and so alone has been.

The Easiest Demise

Zeev Kachel, 1993

Oh Wind, where will you carry me
Toward what fate, what shore, what bay?
Will I be dropped to an open sea
Or else become an eagle's prey?

For what is death? I can't tell
How beastly, really, might it be?
They say that death will never fell
A young-old person such as me.

And so, who knows? I have no answer
No need to trust all those deceits,
Lift me slowly, oh wind, oh mother
Or I'll take cover under sheets

Perhaps it's better to seek protection
Across the ocean, in a distant town?
I have a passport, a profession
Can apply some makeup, like a clown

On the other hand, to live forever

Is not so good and not preferred,

And it's not written in any charter

What in my life still lies ahead

All my acquaintances have long expired

For me, I think, it is a sin,

To be the last one is undesired

I do not wish to lose my kin

So if to die, then with no haggling

I choose the easiest demise,

A prayer, "God is full of pity"

A headstone for a modest price

With a rotating slab of granite!

A splendid cantor, a deep voice too,

The two trees, I say, cut down, just cut

And let them not obscure my view.

Here's how I wish to be interred:

No eulogy at the graveside plot,

Not nude; but with a flag, thus covered

And never mind the proper spot

Across a stunning slab of granite

My name inscribed in golden letters

There's my poem, and my portrait

A funeral procession during stormy hours

The largest crowd with scores of cars

Pretty women sob in abundant grief

Wiping their nose with a handkerchief.

Obituaries in the newspaper

Some large, some small, both bold and dainty,

And that is all. And with no torture.

For now just bring me a cup of tea.

Bent over Memories

Zeev Kachel, 1988

No longer will I carry you in my arms, little girl
You grew up fast. And daddy's back has bent.
    You learned to walk by yourself
Yet for me you'll always remain a baby
Even though you've spread your wings, left the nest
And your own nest built, somewhere out there.

Now I am alone.
    Supported by memories...
Sitting in the park for hours
    Watching someone else's children.
Time ticks slowly
    But it vanishes fast!
And a seagull up above
    Soars overhead
Oh, white-winged seagull
    Carry my prayer
Faraway over the interval
    To the roof shielding my daughter.

I Plucked a Wildflower

Zeev Kachel, 1993

I plucked a wildflower from my resting place
And it was blue, as if it wore my name, my face
But I was startled suddenly by a snake
Who slinked across the path with one tail shake

I plucked a wildflower from my grave, behind
And in silence, my daughter came to mind
Where are you now? The wave swept you away
In a velvety evening, an eve of dew and ray

I was penetrated by a pouring rain
And for a moment, somehow, I felt alive again
Sensing me, the worms began to rave
I plucked a wildflower from my grave.

And a chorus of crickets kicked off a singsong
Climbing up the wall I danced away, so long!
There's no death in life, no need to feel so sad,
I would've come back already if it were all that bad

There were a few I didn't know among the mourners

I asked myself where they came from, what far corners

The crowd was small, such pity! Some were sad

To those who cried, I smiled and waved a tad.

I left countless bills behind me, heavy debts

Come over, I'll pay them back, you bet!

I stare at you across the big divide

With obvious advantage: no interest on this side

The Heart of Space

Zeev Kachel, 1989

I 've laid down on my back
And a horizontal logic
Dictates its stages.
I shut my eyes
To watch my life, from lows to highs
Go through its changes.
Amidst the nightly surge
I see myself submerge
Afloat at the heart of space.
With neither left or right
Above, or down at base
Time is about to take
Its casualties.
No seasons and no fighting
Only dead silence hiding
Its fallacies.
The film of its changes
Plays out with no stop.
And with no sign, no cue,
In secret it starts to throb
The future, breaking through

I Live Here on Paint and on Toxoid

Zeev Kachel, 1992

I live here on paint and on toxoid

My step faltering, against walls, against barriers

Around me I see nature destroyed

Replaced by some structures for settlers.

I live here with no joy, no regret

And scribble little rhymes just for me

I live... No longer preach at the gate,

Nor squash any ants carelessly.

In their hiding place they seem to await

And observe me, in all probability.

I live with no account and no friend

No longer try to right wrongs in the world,

I cannot tell my future, my end

Simply listen to the waves, to my heart.

At set, prescribed times I just swallow

Pills encoded by various pigments

And let my mind labor to follow

The secret paths of this universe.

It is clear to me now: There is no amity

There has never been any beginning,

And all that is here, that is growing

Was here and it always will be.

In space there is no upper or lower

No right and no left all around,

The moment is here—no past, no forever

There is no first, no last or well-found.

Only an unending, unstoppable flow

And shapes that are shifting at will

There is no heaven, only hell and owe

There is time, there is space, there is still.

There is no happiness, no sorrow, no feeling

Only waves dancing without and within

In a struggle with no hatred, no foaming

Without saints, without angels or sin.

So call this entirety: Yin.

The Time is Near

Zeev Kachel, 1989

The time is near
The verdict—known

I have no fear

I shall go alone

Fall

Zeev Kachel, 1989

Encircled by leaves, flying
I'm afloat at last
Somewhere a fire's dying
Anther day about to pass

Autumn's Gold

Zeev Kachel, 1989

A utumn's gold is dripping from the trees
And no one's gathering it
Golden light escaping through my fingers, no way to seize
No point in chasing it

On My Body

Zeev Kachel, 2000

On my body, time leaves its traces
On my body, time jots down its warnings
My heart is throbbing—when will it stop?
In it, time carves its phrases
Time writes its verdict, then on it paces.

Tired of Fighting

Zeev Kachel, 2000

T ired of battles, I wish to take a rest
   Under a green, lush tree
I'll lie down, stretch and fall asleep in the bosom of Time,
   And the wind shall caress me
And when the dream comes I'll say, now I see!
Sweet vision, let me reach for you, embrace me as I dream.

It All Passes

Zeev Kachel

I t all passes: teacher after teacher,
Parents, childhood, pain of knowledge,
Friendship, love, with its fever
School, going abroad, then college,
Hunger, jobs of odds and ends
Trying hard to earn dough
Girls, women come and go...
Finally silence here descends

It all passes: the good, the bad
Family, brothers, sisters,
Meetings, farewells, glad and sad
Enemies, war after war
Hate, loathing, victims, gore
And dreams of something you can't reach
For peace to come, not just in speech
Despite the criminal acts of war
Despite the hatred for no reason
Dreams of prophets' vision for
Our heritage in a future season

Maybe

Zeev Kachel, 1989

Maybe I'll never reach the shore

The shore, perhaps, never existed for me

And the dream that I carried, that dream may call for

Someone else to discover a new land, a new sea

My hour may not have arrived yet, I'm worried.

The seed that I planted has been blown off by a gust

But this I know: the dream that I carried

Will take root, it shall come to full blossom, it must

Maybe I would leave here peculiar, unknown,

Those of small stature would ignore me, these days

But my poem, the one that was torn and blown

One of these days shall set all ablaze

Perhaps

Zeev Kachel, 1989

Perhaps poems would promise you nothing

Perhaps poems are just a waste of time

Perhaps the audience would deem them not fit to sing

And try to define something else as sublime.

Perhaps I'll be left here bald-headed, alone

And no one will even remember my name

But a yearning shall remain for something unknown

And a search, never weary, for what's far from the same

Perhaps they will wrap with my poem a herring

Unable to sense which one yields the flavor; and with force

They will cast me right back into the sea, sparing

Me, somehow, as a matter of course

Maybe

Zeev Kachel, 2001

M aybe my boat shall never reach the shore

Maybe I'll be forced down, into the abyss

Or maybe I'll emerge, and with a sudden roar

Unload my burden; no more of this.

Vigil Light

Zeev Kachel, 1988

I lit a vigil light in the heart of men,
So they'll find the path once I am gone,
The grass will whisper a the words of my poem then
The most alluring star will signal before dawn

At last the hardships of my journey will abate
And in space I'll drift for a long, long run
Upon my resting place, a pale moon will dilate
And wolves will wail, calling out for the lone one.

Because I praised the beauty in what's human
Blue dust of stars will inscribe my name
An eternal vault I erected in the heart of men
The wick of my candle shall be set aflame

I scattered words around me, with no regrets
While rocks laid heavy, heavy on my heart
I let fly the sparks of my soul, my poems, my vignettes
And so I'm left here, naked and apart.

A Memorial

Zeev Kachel, 1992

I have erected a memorial for myself in the heart of men
It won't crumble, as long as on the morrow
Someone will come to feel my pain, and then
Will strive to solve the universal sorrow

Then like diamonds, my tears will shine
And blind my enemies wherever they may be
The words I wrote in silence, line by line
Will point the way for every dreamer, there to see

You'll always find a spot of muck, on any surface
Another parasite who feeds upon your strength
Don't retreat, my friend, just don't be nervous
Under the glass, even a leech seems magnified in length

They will disappear without a trace, a smidgen
You and your poem will continue to excite
Because your truth, the truth that they have hidden
A young person will come, and bring to light[5].

---

[5] In Hebrew, *bring to light* has also the meaning: *publish*

A Lone Wolf

Zeev Kachel, 1989

When I will no longer be, my paintings will speak for me

And my poems—

When I will no longer be—

My absence will speak for me

When I will no longer be.

And then—

You will say:

He was a good man, but an angry one

A man of quarrel and strife.

He was one-of-a-kind.

He flew by like a bird

Very separate. Distinct.

And severe.

It's a pity he's gone.

A lone wolf.

Time Crawls Slowly

Zeev Kachel, 1989

Time crawls slowly but it flies by fast

Up there on the hilltop my torch is ablaze at last

About to flow away to a stormy sea, I start

With everyone else around me, but somehow set apart

Fantasy

Zeev Kachel

Could it be this has been nothing but fantasy

I recall what has never occurred till today?

Could the bright colors I painted so elaborately

On a pink canvas be reduced to a gray?

Is this really the path I envisioned?

Then why is the night here so black?

Was the poem I nearly abandoned

A prayer for a light, for a new track?

Each journey is dictated by some power

And if you stray, fate corrects you, in full motion

Why, then, did I pluck, pluck that flower

Which is beautiful, yet dripping with poison?

Has our life reached its end already

Has our dream collapsed, all carved up?

Our home raided, it's broken, unsteady

The sounds of yearning silenced, hushed up?

Blessed

Zeev Kachel, 1988

I'm blessed for the pleasure, blessed for the agony
Blessed for the fear, the pain of it all
In which I was steeped, in this reality
I was granted the chance to endure or to fall

I'm blessed for the hardship, and blessed for the hurt
Blessed for the crevices, obstacles and all
In the heart of the storm, my journey I chart
To leap over the inferno, and turn back to recall

I'm blessed to have lived, in honor and courage
Blessed I could take a deep plunge, then soar
Blessed for the vinegar, and blessed for the honey
Blessed to be counted with the few at the fore
That somehow did reach their big destiny.

In a Dark Night with not a Friend

Zeev Kachel, 2001

In a dark night with not a friend
I walked all alone in the world
A splitting burst of thunder I heard
And sea breakers that hammered and curled.

A thunder rolled over the skies
Wind gusts battered me with a cry
Terror blinded my eyes
I couldn't tell an enemy from an ally.

In a night with not a friend, all bleary
I could see no shelter around
I walked on, broken and weary
Searching for hope to be found

I Am

Zeev Kachel

I am water, I am fire
I am poem, I inspire
I am silence, sound, a pen stroke
I am blue, a twist of smoke.

About the Cover & Illustrations

When my father passed away, I went back home for the traditional Shiva-a, the seven days period of mourning. Perhaps the grief did something to change the way I viewed things, or else it was sitting in that space—my childhood home—in a spot I rarely sat before, discovering it from a new angle, observing how light penetrated the far reaches of this place, how the furniture signified relationships in the family. I drew what I saw on a napkin; wiped my tears with it, and later discarded it.

Coming back to the states, I recreated that sketch from memory. In my new drawing I used a fish-eye perspective. What does that mean? Like regular perspective, the horizontal lines converge into a vantage point in the distance. But here is the difference: the vertical lines are not straight, nor are they parallel. As you look up, vertical lines converge to a point up there, beyond the edge of the paper. You can call it Heaven. And as you look down, the vertical lines converge to a point below, call it Hell. Which makes the entire perspective embrace you, as if you are in the middle of a fish bowl, seeing the world curve around you.

And looking though such a perspective, what did I see? An earthquake, really, in the aftermath of my father's death. Books falling off the shelves; the lamp swinging like a pendulum; the little side table (in the front) overturned, so my father will never lay his pen upon it; and instead of the persian rugs that used to adorn this space once upon a time, I floated blank pages on the floor; pages he will never again use for writing.

In my next sketch I let the lamp swing even higher into the air. The place has completely tilted, and my father's armchair is ascending above the rest of the furniture. This is the sketch I used for an oil painting called My Father's Armchair, which later became the cover of this book.

About this Book

*H**ome.* A simple word; a loaded one. You can say it in a whisper; you can say it in a cry. Expressed in the voices of father and daughter, you can hear a visceral longing for an ideal place, a place never to be found again.

Imagine the shock, imagine the sadness when a daughter discovers her father's work, the poetry he had never shared with anyone during the last two decades of his life. Six years after that moment of discovery, which happened in her childhood home while mourning for his passing, Uvi Poznansky presents a tender tribute: a collection of poems and prose, half of which is written by her, and half—by her father, the author, poet and artist Zeev Kachel. She has been translating his poems for nearly a year, with careful attention to rhyme and rhythm, in an effort to remain faithful to the spirit of his words.

Zeev's writing is always autobiographical in nature; you can view it as an ongoing diary of his life. Uvi's writing is rarely so, especially when it comes to her prose. She is a storyteller who delights in conjuring up various figments of her imagination, and fleshing them out on paper. She sees herself chasing her characters with a pen, in an attempt to see the world from their point of view, and to capture their voices. But in some of her poems, she offers you a rare glimpse into her most guarded, intensely private moments, yearning for *Home.*

About Zeev Kachel

Zeev Kachel, an author, poet and artist, published three books during his lifetime: a prose book *Dams Erupting* published in 1957, offering a personal account of events during his captivity in Jordan during Israel's war of independence in 1948; a poetry book *Can We Still Love* published in 1961, questioning our capability to give and receive love, having witnessed the inhumanity of two world wars; and a poetry book *Beyond The Window, What Day Is It Today,* published in 1977, bringing to light an unusual creative collaboration with his daughter, Uvi Poznansky. Now after all these years, *Home* celebrates once again the spirit—and the action—of joining forces.

Until his passing in 2006 at the age of ninety four, Zeev created a prolific body of work. His attention alternated frequently between painting and writing. He left the fancy, 'poetic' words behind, his craft becoming increasingly direct, and deeply personal. He archived his latest poems; they were never published in his lifetime. During the mourning period for his passing, his daughter found a treasure in his apartment: stacks and stacks of notes, stories, plays and poems, never before shared with anyone. He had written them out of pain, in response to his separation from his wife at the age of seventy.

A selection of these poems was offered in the original language, in the book *Ropes, Separation, Tear,* edited and published by his daughter six years after his death. The opening poems in the book harken back to his childhood, describing the pain[6] of growing up in eastern Europe, struggling to survive in the face of hate and antisemitism.

---

[6] In Hebrew, the word *ropes* means *cords*, but also *pain*, as in *growing pain*.

The following poems talk about separation, expressing a sense of betrayal, loneliness and despair.

The closing poems describe an emotional rip, a tear from life. For many years, he had been waiting for death, thinking about it all the while. Perhaps in the end he came close to meeting it with a degree of acceptance.

In the last few months, his daughter has been translating the poems from Hebrew. Offering them here, in *Home*, she kept them in the same order as in *Ropes*, *Separation*, *Tear*, inviting you to take the same emotional journey.

About Uvi Poznansky

Uvi Poznansky is a *USA TODAY* bestselling, award-winning author, poet and artist. "I paint with my pen," she says, "and write with my paintbrush."

Uvi earned her B. A. in Architecture and Town Planning from the Technion in Haifa, Israel. During her studies and in the years immediately following her graduation, she practiced with an innovative Architectural firm, taking part in the design of a large-scale project, *Home for the Soldier*.

Having moved to Troy, N.Y. with her husband and two children, Uvi received a Fellowship grant and a Teaching Assistantship from the Architecture department at Rensselaer Polytechnic Institute. There, she guided teams in a variety of design projects and earned her M.A. in Architecture. Then, taking a sharp turn in her education, she earned her M.S. degree in Computer Science from the University of Michigan.

During the years she spent in advancing her career—first as an architect, and later as a software engineer, software team leader, software manager and a software consultant (with an emphasis on user interface for medical instruments devices)—she wrote and painted constantly. In addition, she taught art appreciation classes.

Her versatile body of work can be seen in two websites: her <u>blog</u> includes thoughts about the creative process, reader reviews, author interviews, excerpts from her novels, voice clips from her audiobooks, poems and short stories. Her <u>art site</u> includes bronze and ceramic sculptures, paper engineering projects, oil and watercolor paintings, charcoal, pen and pencil drawings, and mixed media.

Coma Confidential, Overkill, Overdose, and *Overdue* are novels in the *Ash Suspense Thrillers with a Dash of Romance* series. With each new case, Ash uses grit and intuition to solve the crime.

Virtually Lace is the first volume in a multi-author thriller series, *High-Tech Crime Solvers*, where the authors bring each other's characters into their books.

My Own Voice, The White Piano, The Music of Us, Dancing with Air, and *Marriage before Death* are novels in the *Still Life with Memories* series, a family saga with a love story that develops in the face of hardship and illness over two generations, starting at the 1980's, then harkening back to WWII when Lenny, a soldier, and Natasha, a rising star, first met. These books are also offered in two bundles: *Apart from Love* and *Apart from War*.

Rise to Power, A Peek at Bathsheba, and *The Edge of Revolt* are novels in *The David Chronicles*, telling the story of David as you have never heard it before: from the king himself, telling the unofficial version, the one he never allowed his court scribes to recount. In his mind, history is written to praise the victorious—but at the last stretch of his illustrious life, he feels an irresistible urge to tell the truth. These books are also offered in a trilogy.

In addition, *The David Chronicles* includes six art collections: *Inspired by Art: Fighting Goliath, Inspired by Art: Fall of a Giant, Inspired by Art: Rise to Power, Inspired by Art: A Peek at Bathsheba, Inspired by Art: The Edge of Revolt,* and *Inspired by Art: The Last Concubine*.

A Favorite Son, a new-age twist on an old yarn, is inspired by the biblical story of Jacob and his mother Rebecca, plotting together against the elderly father Isaac, who is lying on his deathbed.

Twisted is a unique collection, laden with shades of mystery. Here, you will come into a dark, strange world, a hyper-reality where nearly everything is firmly rooted in the familiar—except for some quirky detail that twists the yarn.

Home, Uvi's deeply moving poetry book in tribute of her father, includes her poetry and prose, as well as translated poems from the pen of her father, the poet and author Zeev Kachel.

Uvi wrote and illustrated two children's books, *Jess and Wiggle* and *Now I Am Paper*. Watch the beautiful animations she created for these books on YouTube.

A Note to the Reader

Thank you for reading this book! I hope you enjoyed it. If you did, I invite you to check out more books from the same pen. There is always a new project on my drawing board, so come back to check it out.

I would love to hear what you thought of this book. You have the power of bringing it to the attention of more readers, by posting your own review. It would mean so much to me.

And another thing you can do to help me spread the word is this: please tell your friends about my work. How else will they hear about the story? How else will the characters, who sprang from my mind onto these pages, leap from there into new minds?

Bonus Excerpts
Excerpt: The Music of Us

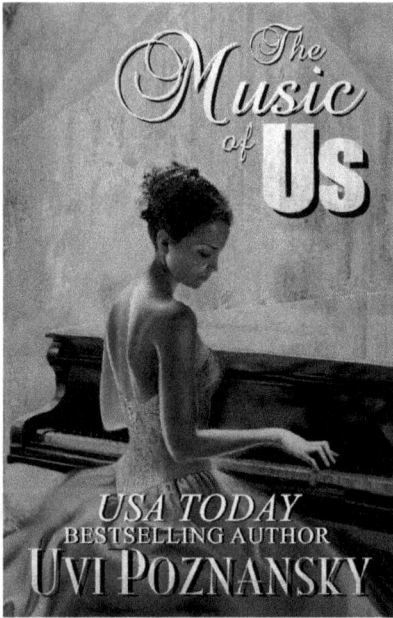

My son, Ben, has been gone for a month now, staying in some youth hostel in Rome. If I call him, if I stumble into revealing how scared I am that his mother is losing her mind, he may listen. He may heed my fears, grudgingly, and come back here, not even knowing how to offer his support to me. Should I ask for it?

The last thing I wish to do is lean on him for help. He is not strong enough, and whatever the problem may be with her, I can grit my teeth and handle it, somehow, all by myself. Besides, I pray for a spontaneous change in her. I mean, her memory may take a turn for the better just as quickly as it has deteriorated.

Given this hope I decide that for now I will not schedule the head X-Ray that her doctor recommended for her. I figure she has been through so many checkups, so many exams to rule out depression, vitamin B deficiency, and a long list of other possible ailments, all of which has been in vain.

So far, the results have failed to produce a conclusive diagnosis, and this new X-Ray will be no different, because from what I have read, Alzheimer's disease can be determined only through autopsy, by linking clinical measures with an examination of brain tissue. So this new medical hypothesis is just that: a hypothesis. One that cannot be proven; one that cannot go away. An ever-present threat.

Perhaps all she needs is rest. Time, I tell myself. I must give her time. Meanwhile I resolve to keep her condition secret from everyone, especially from my son. Let him enjoy his time away from home, his independence.

Since his departure I called him only once, three weeks ago, and said little, except for blurting out the mundane, "How's Rome?"

"Great," he said vaguely, adding no particulars.

I could not help myself from asking. "So, what about your plans?"

"What about them?"

"D'you have any?"

"For now I have none," he admitted, and immediately changed the subject. "How's mom?"

"Fine."

"Is she?"

"She is," I lied, hoping that the sound of my voice would not betray the tensing of my muscles, the tightening of my jaws.

"Oh good," he said. "Really, really good."

There is only one thing more difficult than talking to Ben, and that is writing to him. Amazingly, having to conceal what his mother is going through makes every word—even on subjects unrelated to her —that much harder. I find myself oppressed by my own self-imposed discipline, the discipline of silence.

And what can I tell him, really? That I keep digging into the past, mining its moments, trying to piece them together this way and that, dusting off each memory of Natasha, of how we were, the highs and lows of the music of us, to find out where the problem may have started?

To him, that may seem like an exercise in futility. For me, it is a necessary process of discovery, one that is as tormenting as it is delightful. If the dissonance in our life would fade away, so will the harmony.

Sometimes I go as far back as the moment we first met, when I was a soldier and she—a star, brilliant yet illusive. Natasha was a riddle to me then, and to this day, with all the changes she has gone through, she still is.

I often wonder: can we ever understand, truly understand each other—soldier and musician, man and woman, one heart and another? Will we ever again dance together to the same beat? Is there a point where we may still touch?

Excerpt: Dancing with Air

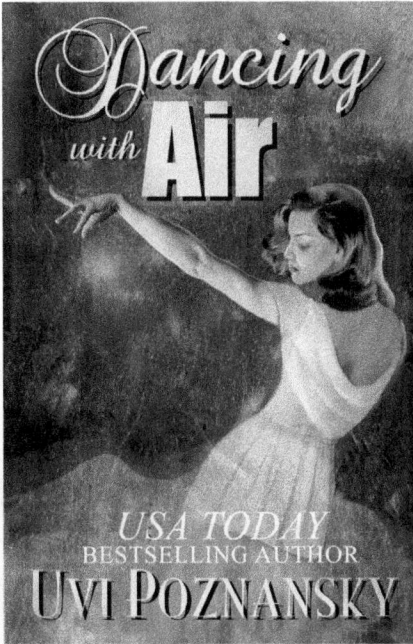

Overcome, suddenly, by exhaustion, Natasha stepped out of my embrace and plopped onto her suitcase. "Ma came to say goodbye, " she said. "I saw her across from me, as we left the shore. She was offering a prayer, tears running down her cheeks. Then, once out to sea, the Germans fired at us."

"Really? What happened?"

"The ships, they took up their positions in the convoy and plodded ahead. Straightaway, two of them were lost. One ran aground. The other, suffering from engine trouble, turned back to the harbor. And as for us I thought that was the end."

I shuddered at the thought.

"This journey," said Natasha, "it was more challenging than anything I've gone through in the past. Even watching Papa during his last months was easier, in a way, because back then I was on the outside, observing his pain."

I waited for her to continue.

After a slight reflection, she added, "I could only guess what was happening to him, I mean, the ways his illness drained his mind, the ways he suffered. But now, I wasn't an observer. I lived it, Lenny! Everyone on board—including me—was going through the same fear, the same hardship."

I could not help but ask her, "What were you thinking, putting yourself at risk?"

In reply, she rose to her feet. "For this very moment," she said, clinging to me, "I would go through it all over again."

I took a step back, to stress, "Your Mama, she's beside herself with worry, and as for me—"

"You talked to her?" asked Natasha, her eyes twinkling. "Of course you did, how else would you know to wait here for me? She doesn't get it—"

"And neither do I!"

"But Lenny, it's so simple! I missed you—"

"That's no reason, Natasha, for what you've done. Why leave home, especially now, when we're at war? If you love me, keep yourself safe, if only for my sake! Why, why put your life at risk—"

"Perhaps," she said, "I'm not looking for safety! Have you ever thought of that? Perhaps something else is more important to me."

"Like what?"

"I can't continue to depend on others, Lenny, the way I've done all my life. This is my time to change, to demand new things of myself, even if they happen to frighten me, even if I'm scared out of my mind."

"Not sure I understand—"

"Please try, Lenny."

"What is it you want?"

"Just this: to stop leaning on those closest to me."

"You could've done that back home, couldn't you?"

"That's the place where I'm being taken care of, to the point of feeling stuck. Worse than that: suffocated. Someone, usually Mama, drives me to where I need to be. Someone points me to the dressing room, calls me to the stage. I'm nothing more than a mechanical doll. All I do is respond."

"You do much more than that! You excite audiences, Natasha! And to me, you're an inspiration—"

"Yes, you admire the way I play, but in truth music is the only thing for which Papa trained me."

"You're too critical of yourself," I said.

To which she said, "No, Lenny. I've seen him decline, seen him lose his mind, and if—if, like him, I'll ever lose mine—how in the world will I recover? How will I find my way, when I've never developed the skill to do so?"

I lowered my head before her.

"Never," I said, "until now."

"Exactly," said Natasha. "Until now."

And a moment later, blotting the corner of her eye, where a tear was forming, she whispered to me, "Come closer, Lenny, snuggle up, but never, ever let me lean on you."

Excerpt: A Peek at Bathsheba

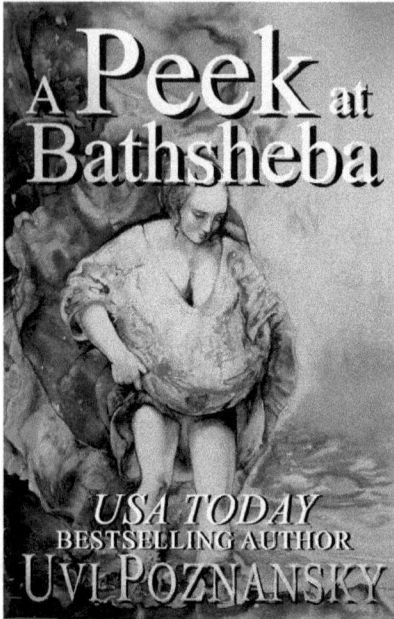

Wrapped in a long, flowing fabric that creates countless folds around her curves, she loosens just the top of it and lets it slide off her head—only to reveal a blush, and mischievous glint, shining in her eye. It is over that sparkle that I catch a sudden reflection, coming from the back window, of a full moon.

Looking left, right, and down the staircase, to make sure no one is lurking outside my chamber door, I let her in. Then I lock it behind her, so no one may intrude upon us.

In a manner of greeting I raise my goblet. It is a gift from my supplier, Hiram king of Tyre, and unlike the other goblets I have in my possession, this one is made of fine glass, with minute air bubbles floating in it. With a big splash I fill it up to the rim with red, aromatic wine. In it I dip a glistening, ruddy cherry, and offer it to her, with a flowery toast.

"For you," I say. "With my everlasting love!"

Bathsheba takes the goblet from my hand, and raises it to her lips. "Love, everlasting?" she says, raising an eyebrow. "What does that mean, in this place?"

I hesitate to ask, "What place is that?"

"This court," she says, with a slight curtsy, "where the signature feature is a harem, which is as big as the king is endowed with glory."

"Glory is a good thing," say I, lowering my voice. "But sometimes it is better to meet in the shadows."

"Especially," she says, matching her voice to mine, "when there are so many others."

"Here we are," say I. "It's just us."

"Really," says Bathsheba, sipping her wine and ever so delightfully, licking her lips. "It must be a special night, then! Just you and me, and no one else, no one else at all."

Yet I cannot avoid feeling the presence of someone other than me in her thoughts, perhaps her husband, Uriah, who is one of my mighty soldiers and the most trusty of them. Earlier today he must have received his transfer orders to join the cavalry in the eastern hills, where he would be stationed outside the city of Rabbah.

I have a catch in my throat as I tell her, "I'm so glad you came."

Bathsheba lifts her eyes and looks straight at me.

"Really," she says, in her most velvety tone. "You mean, I had a choice in this matter?"

Her question stumps me at first, because how can I admit that she is right, so right in asking it? Instead I just shrug.

"You do have a choice," I say at last. "And I hope you'll make it."

"I'm so glad to hear that," says Bathsheba. "With that ape, I mean, that bodyguard of yours knocking so loudly, so rudely, and for such a long time at my door, I had my doubts about it."

"You can go, if you wish," I stress, with a reluctant tone. "But I wish you wouldn't. Stay with me, tonight."

Bathsheba picks the stem of the red cherry, and takes little bites out of it. In her pleasure she hums, and smacks her lips. Then she raises the goblet to my lips, letting me take in the aroma. I do, and then I take a long gulp.

With a slight sway of her hips Bathsheba walks past me, knowing I cannot take my eyes off of her. She wanders about my chamber as if she were the one owning it.

"You've been brought here by my order," I whisper to her, across the space. "But I am the one held captive."

Excerpt: Overkill

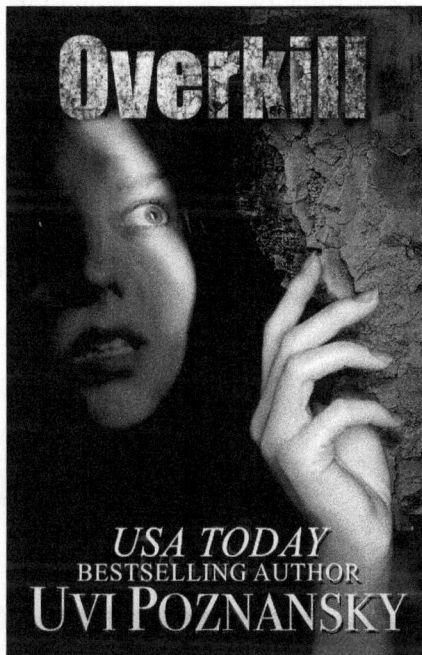

Ed lies still on the sidewalk, his eyelids open but unflinching. The only thing about him that moves are the lapels of his corduroy coat, flapping slightly this way and that across his neck as the wind floats chilly feelers over his body.

Timmy gasps—but his eyes are not tearful, not yet. In that second, when time slows, the driver side door is swaying with an annoying noise. With each squeak, the child takes a gulp of air as if about to ask, "Dad, will you get up? Will you grab the door handle?"

No blood is visible, at first. So, I too allow myself to wonder: Will Ed climb back into his seat, dust off his shoulders, and wave goodbye to his son, before driving away?

I expect him to do so. Almost.

Until another round of gunshots blasts the air.

Without even thinking, I push Timmy down to the asphalt, which is quite easy because he's such a skinny child and utterly in shock. Then I land hard on my elbows beside him and push a hand against his chest until he crawls backwards, until he butts against his father's car.

It casts a shadow over him. At the moment, there is no better place to hide.

Up on the pavement, a short distance from us, blood starts puddling around Ed's shoulder. I try to block Timmy from seeing it.

He shakes his head, still in disbelief.

Please, God, no. This can't be true.

Everything around us is in a state of utter confusion. The sidewalk is strewn with abandoned backpacks, as some pupils are running for their lives. Others cower behind a bush or a car. One uses his flimsy umbrella as a shield.

A teacher cries out to him, "Duck!"

And another teacher, by the gate of the school, yells, "Run! Get inside! Get down, crawl under your desks! And for Heaven's sake, stay away from the windows!"

A couple of parents attempt getting out of their cars to pull their children to safety, but at the sound of shooting they drop to their knees with empty arms.

Next to me, Timmy turns onto his stomach, mashes his nose against the tire, and wedges himself, somehow, between the curb and the Ford. Then he crawls under it toward the rear bumper, making room for me, too.

I try to cock my head up from the damp surface. Looking at the scene from under the belly of a car is a whole different experience. Someone stands at the other side of the car, and all I can see is his sneakers, socks, and the hem of his coat, flaring at its bottom. Also, the muzzle of his gun. For a heartbeat, before dark clouds close in, it glints in the sunlight.

I reach over and clamp a hand over Timmy's mouth to prevent him from screaming, from drawing the killer's attention. A hail of bullets rains down, sparking off the front bumper.

Timmy tenses up. His breath trembles as it escapes my touch. I must protect him. I must bring him back safely to his mother.

The edge of the curb gouges into my back. I adjust, I turn over. Now it presses against my belly.

I must not lose this child, either.

Now, the killer kicks the grill of the car, then jams his weapon, hard, into the front window. I know it by seeing only one of his feet on the ground and by the sound of cracking. It reverberates all over as the car shakes. Shards of glass come pinging against the asphalt and stab at my fingers.

Why is he wasting his time—at the risk of being identified, or even caught—on an empty car, when all around us, juicier targets come into his view?

Excerpt: Virtually Lace

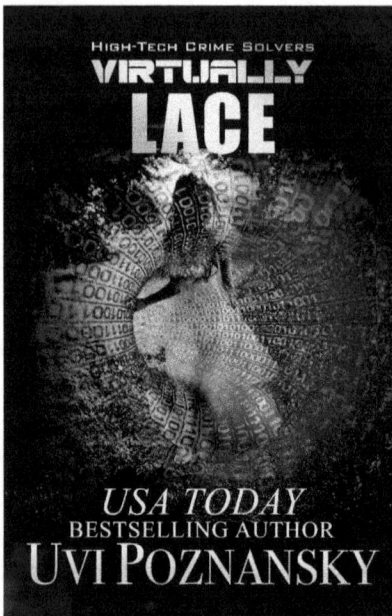

E ven before Michael spotted the body, the idea of creating a simulation of the scene occurred to him. At sunset, the panoramic view of Laguna Beach was awe-inspiring. He wondered if he could render it convincingly in his model, the virtual reality model which he had been developing in the back of his garage for months, until the recent acquisition of his software by a military ops company.

Could beauty be taken apart without loss of emotional impact?

Could its data be synthesized, somehow, into a lifelike experience? In short, could he apply his analytical skills to fool his own senses?

For now, these were purely academic questions. They occupied his mind, which helped him forget his loneliness. Michael brought his car to a stop at the corner of Cliff Drive and let it maneuver by itself into a tight parking spot. In all probability, this evening would be uneventful, or so he thought. It was the end of April. He had nothing to do and no one to do it with.

Sitting there awhile, lost in his thoughts, how was he to know that in the coming days he was going to revisit this place, starting at this particular intersection, to examine every possible angle, every conceivable point of view?

The shadow of the lamppost grew longer. It prowled over to the pavement on the other side, where it lost its sharpness. The evening breeze turned overhead with a shriek, only to fall into a whoosh. Michael imagined it whispering, of all things, of murder at dusk. What a crazy idea! Where did that come from?

At 8:03pm came the sound of footfalls. A teenage girl was walking down the street so fast that the uneven click of her heels was already passing him by, leaving a faint whiff of perfume. No, that must have been some other fragrance, perhaps the saltiness of the sea, drifting over the sweetness of creek milkweeds and Belladonna lilies.

Where had he seen her before?

By the time he got out of the car, the girl had already crossed to the other side. With each step, the white dress whipped across her legs and fluttered, fold upon fold, in the cold wind.

His soles beat an echo in the empty street. He didn't mind the occasional squeak, because he had just bought them.

Electric lights buzzed in the buildings behind him, and foxtail ferns hissed, swaying along the trail. Her shadow flitted over the shrubs, falling farther and farther out of reach.

Before reaching the bend, she glanced over her shoulder and for a heartbeat, met his eyes. In some ways she reminded him of his ex-girlfriend, Ash, whom he hadn't seen since the *incident*. What was it that drew him to this girl? Why was he looking, time and again, to save a damsel in distress?

There was a certain quality about that look, which he couldn't put into words. Anguish? No, it was more acute than that. The closest he could name it was fear.

Excerpt: Twisted

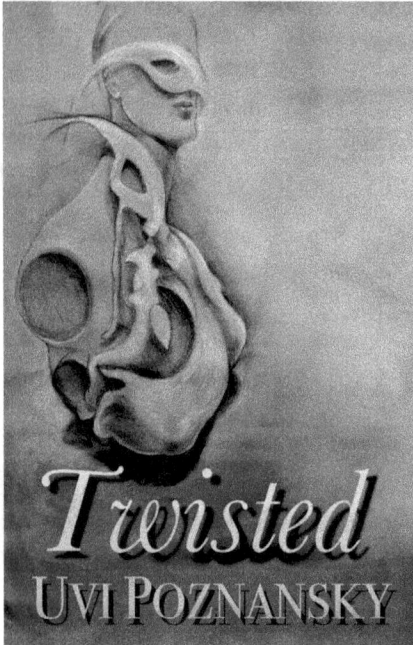

He turns to me with a sly look. To my surprise, his smile—even with those sharp fangs—is quite endearing.

"Job's wife, I presume? Hallelujah! I have been expecting you for quite a long while," says Satan. His voice is sweet. He must have sung in a choir in his youth, because in some ways he sounds as pious as my husband. "Shame, shame, shame on you," he wags his finger. "You sure made me wait, didn't you..."

And without allowing time for an answer, he brings a magnifying glass to his bloodshot eye. Enlarged, his pupil is clearly horizontal and slit-shaped.

Which makes me feel quite at home with him, because so are the pupils of the goats in the herds we used to own.

Meanwhile, Satan unfolds a piece of paper and runs his finger through some names listed there. Then, with a gleam of satisfaction he marks a checkbox there, right in the middle of the crinkled page. At once, a whiff of smoke whirls in the air.

Satan blows off a few specks of charred paper, folds the thing and tucks it into his breast pocket, somewhere in his wool. Cashmere, I ask myself? Really? In this heat?

Back home, when I would count my gold coins, this was something I craved with a passion... It would keep me warm during the long winter nights...

Then, without even bothering to look at me, Satan says, "I swear, madam, you look lovely tonight."

For a moment I am grateful that my husband is among the living. Or so I think. Nowadays, influenced by the elders, he regards swearing as a mortal sin, as bad as cursing. He even plugs his ears, for no better reason than to avoid hearing it. But if you ask me, I swear: without a bit of blasphemy, language would utterly dull, and fit for nothing but endless prayer. Sigh.

Strangely, Satan does not frighten me that much anymore. And so, swaying on my hip bones, I strut out of the cave in his direction. I feel an odd urge to fondle his horns. Along the path toward him I make sure to suck in my belly, because in the company of a gentleman, even a corpse is entitled to look her best.

Books by Uviart

Coma Confidential

(Volume I of *Ash Suspense Thrillers with a Dash of Romance*)

Kindle: B07L92YHST Paperback: 978-1791691592

Overkill

(Volume II of *Ash Suspense Thrillers with a Dash of Romance*)

Kindle: B084GDK156 Paperback: 979-8644328192

Overdose

(Volume III of *Ash Suspense Thrillers with a Dash of Romance*)

Kindle: B07VP4S6PK Paperback: 978-1086703665

Overdue

(Volume IV of *Ash Suspense Thrillers with a Dash of Romance*)

Kindle: B08S724T4G Paperback: 979-8599499671

Ash Suspense Thrillers: Trilogy

(Volume I-III of *Ash Suspense Thrillers with a Dash of Romance*)

Kindle: B0893MJNSY Paperback: 979-8648269644

Virtually Lace

(Volume I of *High-Tech Crime Solvers*)

Kindle: B07L968RXD Paperback: 978-1790407187

My Own Voice

(Volume I of *Still Life with Memories*)

Kindle: B013TA3FBS Paperback: 978-0984993215

The White Piano

(Volume II of *Still Life with Memories*)

Kindle: B013TAU7L4 Paperback: 978-1517049447

The Music of Us

(Volume III of *Still Life with Memories*)

Kindle: B013TCYWHC Paperback: 978-0-9849932-9-1

Dancing with Air

(Volume IV of *Still Life with Memories*)

Kindle: B01I4ENROY Paperback: 978-1536896534

Marriage before Death

(Volume V of *Still Life with Memories*)

Kindle: B0746NW5CD Paperback: 978-1974001736

Apart from Love

(*Still Life with Memories Bundle I*)

Kindle: B006WPITP0 Paperback: 978-0-9849932-0-8

Apart from War

(*Still Life with Memories Bundle II*)

Kindle: B07MMZLD7Z Paperback: 978-1792131592

Rise to Power

(Volume I of *The David Chronicles*)

Kindle: B00H6PMZ0U Paperback: 978-0-9849932-4-6

A Peek at Bathsheba

(Volume II of *The David Chronicles*)

Kindle: B00LEPPDV6 Paperback: 978-0-9849932-7-7

The Edge of Revolt

(Volume III of *The David Chronicles*)

Kindle: B00Q5WVKA6 Paperback: 978-0984993284

The David Chronicles: Trilogy

(Volume I-III of *The David Chronicles*)

Kindle: B00QYGF6WG Paperback: 978-1797440699

The David Chronicles: Art

(Volume IV-XI of *The David Chronicles*)

Kindle: B08YWSH7HC Paperback: 979-8721612886

Inspired by Art: Fighting Goliath

(Art book. Volume IV of *The David Chronicles*)

Kindle: B01MSBNSE4   Paperback 978-1797726212

Inspired by Art: Fall of a Giant

(Art book. Volume V of *The David Chronicles*)

Kindle: B01MSBS82Q   Paperback: 978-1092307765

Inspired by Art: Rise to Power

(Art book. Volume VI of *The David Chronicles*)

Kindle: B01N2786VX   Paperback: 978-1092263207

Inspired by Art: A Peek at Bathsheba

(Art book. Volume VII of *The David Chronicles*)

Kindle: B01MUFS9OA   Paperback: 978-1092306225

Inspired by Art: The Edge of Revolt

(Art book. Volume VIII of *The David Chronicles*)

Kindle: B01N6ZG0W8   Paperback: 978-1091306158

Inspired by Art: The Last Concubine

(Art book. Volume IX of *The David Chronicles*)

Kindle: B01N2AXQP2   Paperback: 978-1092302715

A Favorite Son

Kindle: B00AUZ3LGU Paperback: 978-0-9849932-5-3

Twisted

Kindle: B00D7Q3IY4

Paperback: 978-0984993260 Nook: 2940151689588

Home

Kindle: B00960TE3Y

Paperback: 978-09849932-3-9 Nook: 2940151729468

Virtually Yummy: Recipes that Inspire

(Cookbook)

Kindle: B085BDNDM5 Nook: 2940163988655

Apple: id1501182051 Kobo: 9781393589853

בית

(Poetry in Hebrew)
Paperback: 978-1494920968 Nook: 1127367962

Apple: id1302908918 Kobo: 9781540199966

Jess and Wiggle

Kindle: B013D1W0SM Paperback: 978-1494920968

Now I Am Paper

Kindle: B00YQS4O72 Paperback: 978-1494919429